AYATULLAH IBRAHIM AMINI

Principles of Upbringing Children

First published by Ansariyan Publications 1997

Copyright © 1997 by Ayatullah Ibrahim Amini

All rights reserved. No part of this publication may be reproduced, stored or transmitted in any form or by any means, electronic, mechanical, photocopying, recording, scanning, or otherwise without written permission from the publisher. It is illegal to copy this book, post it to a website, or distribute it by any other means without permission.

First edition

Contents

The Translator's Note	1
Foreword	3
The Parent's Responsibility	6
The Knowledge and Mutual Cooperation of the Educators	12
Training Through Deeds, Not Just Talk	16
Abstain from Domestic Differences	20
Starting Life as a Mother	27
Welfare of the Embryo (Fetus) Depends on the Mother's...	30
The Effect of the Mother's Nutrition on the Fetus	32
The Mother's Nutrition	34
Consuming Tobacco	38
When Pregnant Women Fall Ill	41
Effect of the Psychological Condition of the Mother on the...	43
An Advice to Pregnant Women	47
Clean Enviornment	48
Miscarriage	50
Difficult Deliveries	54
After the Birth	59
Mother's Milk - The Best Nutrition	61
Supplement the Mother's Milk	65
Weaning from Mother's Milk	66
The Schedule of Breast Feeding	68
If the Mother is Deficient in Milk	73

Weaning the Child	75
Daughter or Son	77
Naming the Child	80
Health and Hygiene	84
The Child's Sleep and Freedom of Movement	88
The Most Delicate Period of Life	90
The Newborn and Moral Upbringing	93
Religious Upbringing of the Newborn	96
The Sense of Belonging	99
When the Child Starts to See the World Around Him	103
Affection	105
The Expression of Love and Affection	110
Love - Not an Instrument of Convenience	113
Love Should Not Become A Hindrance to Good Upbringing	114
The Spoilt Child	116
Sucking of Thumbs	122
Fear	125
Inane Fears	125
Legitimate Fear	130
Play and Recreation	132
Conceit or Pride	139
Taqleed or Emulation	141
Search for the Truth	144
Self-Confidence	148
Independence	155
Stubbornness	161
Work and Performance of Duties	166
Straightforwardness	173
Keeping Promises	179
Ownership	183
Magnanimity	186

A Helping Hand in Good Work	191
Humaneness and Children	193
Justice and Equality	197
Respect for the Children	202
Self-Assessment and Meaningful Existence	206
The Income of the Household and Expenses	209
Respect for the Law	213
Respect	215
Theft and Kleptomania	219
Jealousy	224
Anger	230
Tongue Lashing and Impertinence	234
Backbiting or Carrying Words	237
Fault-Finding	241
Children's Quarrels	243
Friends and Friendship	249
The Child and Theological Education	254
The Child and the Religious Duties	258
Political and Social Training	262
The Child and the Radio and Television	265
The Gender Problems	272
The Habit of Reading Books	283
Physically Handicapped Children	290
Physical Punishment	294
Non-Physical Punishment	300
Encouragement and Reward	304

The Translator's Note

My friend Riaz Ahmed gave me a copy of the Urdu translation of the book to read and attempt its translation into the English language. He told me that the sponsors are keen to have the book published in the English language for the benet of young, eligible, girls, newly married couples and expectant mothers who do not have prociency in Persian, the language of the original text, nor can they read Urdu in which it has been translated and published.

After reading the book I am convinced that it is a highly commendable project. I feel a copy should reach every household. It should be a part of the dower of newly wed brides, it should be presented to the young married couples and it must be there on every family bookshelf. The book should adorn the bed-side table of every young couple and will be a very useful reference and guide for proper upbringing of children.

Ayatollah *Ustadh* Ibrahim Amini has rightly pointed out in his foreword that the western libraries are chock full of works on child rearing and upbringing, but we nd hardly any comprehensive reference on the subject with particular emphasis on the Islamic norms and guidelines for upbringing of children.

The Western works are more materialistic which emphasize only on the material and moral aspects of child rearing. It is Islam that covers all the aspects including the religious and spiritual guidelines for bringing up the children as good Muslims and citizens. He has extensively quoted from the Holy Book and the Traditions of the Holy Prophet and his Infallible Descendants.

The need for English translations of Islamic works is universally felt and lot of work is being done in this direction. There is a very large section of Muslim youth, although uent at speaking in their native languages, are more comfortable communicating in English which has assumed the status of lingua franca for them.

We also come across people from other faiths who are curious to know more about Islam and they wish to have access to good literature on the subject in the English language. If the publication of the translation of this book sees the light of the day, it will be another small, but signicant step, towards dissemination of Islamic precepts to a wide spectrum of people in the East and the West. *Insha Allah.*

Syed Tahir Bilgrami

Foreword

There is pronounced difference between education and training or upbringing. Education means inculcation of knowledge, or imparting the meanings of the contents of curricula. But upbringing is moulding of personalities on desired lines. The society can be transformed with proper upbringing of its population.

It is imperative that upbringing is based on well thought out program to ensure the degree of desired success. Upbringing is not only sermonizing and admonishing but it requires creation of the right environment towards attainment of the desired results. The criteria necessary for proper upbringing can be listed as:

1. The mentor should be properly acquainted with the student whose upbringing he is assigned to take up. He should familiarize himself with the physical and mental status of the student.
2. The mentor should have dened aims of the training program for the student. The ultimate goal of the upbringing process has to be the development of the student into a humane person.
3. The training program to be inclusive of the desirable criteria

and conditions for producing best results. The mentor then can expect positive results over a period of time.

The best period for commencement of the upbringing or training is the childhood of the student. Childhood is the most impressionable period in the life of a person. At this delicate and responsible juncture the parents can play a very crucial role.

But upbringing of small children is not an easy and simple function and requires deep thought of identication, knowledge, experience, determination and perseverance in the mentor or the parents. It is sad that most parents are found ignorant of the art of upbringing of the children. This is the reason most children are not receiving upbringing on desirable lines and they keep growing like self sustained saplings.

In the progressive countries of the West and the East upbringing of children receives prime importance. They have conducted lot of research in this eld. Many useful books have been published on the subject and they have many experts in the eld. But in our country scant attention has been given to this crucial matter.

We have few knowledgeable persons in this discipline and very few books on the subject which are absolutely insufcient. Quite a few books have been translated from other languages into Persian which are available to people. But these books from the West and the East have two big lacunae.

The rst lacuna is that they treat of only the physical requirement of the students and the stress is on the worldly education of the subjects. All the research rotates around these aspects only and they are totally silent on the spiritual aspect of human life and have ignored any reference to mention of the concept of hereafter.

In the West the only objective is to train the children for their bodies and minds for the attainment of worldly conveniences and pleasures so that when they grow up they have ideal living conditions at their disposal. And if these books deal with the subject of morality they limit themselves to the treatment of morality specic only to the worldly benets and are totally silent about the rewards or retribution which one can earn on the basis of his actions during the worldly life.

The second lacuna is that the training problems in the West are dependence for a solution only on past experiences and statistics. There is no impress of "Faith" in this process. Therefore, these books are not of comprehensive utility for the people of the Muslim Faith. In the eyes of a Muslim the human being has two pronounced aspects—one is the body and the other is the spirit. One pertains to the worldly life and the other to the Hereafter.

In view of this the writer has decided to study and research and thereafter present the conclusions to the seekers of knowledge in the form of a book. For the writing of this book the main source of information has been the Holy The Holy Qur'an, the books of tradition and the writings on moral science.

Reference has also been made to works in Arabic and Persian on the training of children, their psychology, health etc. The books written by Iranian scholars on the upbringing of children were also kept in view. The personal experiences of the author have also been invaluable in this effort. It is hoped that this humble presentation will be of use to the mentors who are associated with the training of impressionable minds in the Muslim community.

Ibrahim Amini Najafabadi
January 1980

The Parent's Responsibility

In the eyes of Islam the status of the father and the mother is very exalted. Allah, the Holy Prophet and the Infallible Imams have exhorted the people in this regard. There are a lot of verses in the Holy Book relevant to the subject. The exemplary behavior of children towards their parents is rated as one of the best invocations. Allah says:

> "Your God has decreed that thou shalt worship only Him and adopt good behavior with (thy) parents." (The Holy Qur'an, 17:23)

Imam Ja'far as-Sadiq observes:
"Three actions are the best: (a) Offer the ve mandatory prayers with punctuality. (b) Maintain good behavior with your parents. (c) Struggle in the cause of Allah.[1]

Now the question arises why this exalted position has been bestowed on the parents of the Faithfull's Allah giving this status for no specic

---

[1] Usul al Ka, book 2, p. 158

reason? What big deed the parents perform for their progeny that they are deemed deserving of the august status. The father, in satisfaction of his carnal desire transfers his sperm into the womb of the mother where it compounds with the ovum and a new being starts to develop and after nine months of the incident arrives into the world as a tiny babe.

The mother suckles it and gives it other nutrition. Sometimes she cleans it and sometimes changes its raiment. She cares of its wetness and dryness. During this time the father takes care of the expenses required for the upkeep of the child.

Don't the parents have any other responsibility besides these? Is it because of performing these duties that the parents have been endowed with the exalted status? Do the parents only have a right over their off-spring and the children don't have any rights over them? In my opinion no one will accept any such one sided privilege. The traditions of the Infallibles of the Holy Prophet's Family are quoted in this regard:

The Holy Prophet of Islam has said: "As your father has a right over you, so does your progeny have a similar right."[2]

The Prophet also said: "As are the children disinherited for their disobedience so also it is possible that the parents may be disowned by the children for not fullling their bonding duties.[3]

The Prophet said: "Allah's curse on such parents who become the cause of disinheriting their children."[4]

Imam Sajjad said: "Your children have a right that you consider if they are good or they are bad. You have been the cause of their birth and the world recognizes them as your offspring. It is your

---

[2] Majma al zawaid, v 8, p. 146

[3] Bihar al-anwar, v 19, p. 93

[4] Makarim al akhlaq, p 518

responsibility that you teach them good manners and guide them toward the recognition and obedience of Allah. Your behavior towards your children must be of a person who believes that a good deed shall get a suitable reward and ill treatment shall call for retribution."[5]

The Commander of the Faithful, 'Ali says: "Beware, your behavior might render your family and your relatives part of the ill fated people."[6]

The Prophet said: "Whoever wishes that his children are safe from disinheritance, he should help them performing good deeds."[7]

The Prophet also said: "To whomsoever a daughter is born should strive to impart norms of good behavior to her and make efforts to educate her. Provide means of comfort to her that she becomes a cause of his deliverance from the Hell Fire.[8]

Above all, Allah says in the Holy The Holy Qur'an:

> "*O, Believers Save yourselves and your dependents from the re whose fuel are humans and the stones." (The Holy Qur'an, 66:6)*

The time when a child is in the process of adopting a way of life which can make him either virtuous or wicked, he can be metamorphosed into a perfect human being or a degraded wild animal. The virtue or wickedness of a person will be dependent on the upbringing he receives and this responsibility rests squarely on the shoulders of the parents.

In fact the parents are instruments of shaping a human being, good

---

[5] Makarim al akhlaq p. 484

[6] Ghurar al hukm, p. 802

[7] Majma al zawaid, v 8, p. 158

[8] Majma al zawaid, v 8, p. 158

or bad, from the child. The greatest service which the parents can render to their children is that they train them to be good mannered, kind, friends of humans, well meaning, freedom loving, bold, just, wise, righteous, noble, faithful, dutiful, hard working, educated.

The parents must mould their children in such a way that they are successful both in the world and hereafter. Only such people are those who are endowed with the exalted status of parenthood, and not those who in fulllment of their carnal desire caused the birth of children and left the children to fend for themselves and rendering them likely to fall into evil ways.

The Holy Prophet said: "The best thing a father provide to his child is good manners and ethical training."[9]

The mother has a more important function to perform towards the upbringing of the progeny. Even during the pregnancy the mother's food habits and her behavior affects the future virtuosity or otherwise of the developing child.

The Prophet of Islam said:

"Lucky is the one whose foundation of his virtue has been made in the womb of the mother and unlucky is one whose wickedness had its rudiments in the mother's womb as well."[10]

"Heaven (i.e. *janna*) is under the feet of one's mother." 1[11]

The parents, who don't pay attention to the education and training of their children, become guilty of gross negligence. Such parents must be asked whether the innocent child pleaded with him to give him birth in the world to be abandoned like sheep and cattle. Now that you have become the cause of his existence, by virtue of religious tenets and human wisdom his education and training is your bonden

---

[9] Majma al zawaid, v 8, p. 159

[10] Bihar al-anwar, v 77, pp. 115-133

[11] Mustadrak al-wasail, v 2, p 38

duty.

The parents are also answerable to the society. Today's children will be men and women, the citizens of tomorrow. The fabric of the society will be made of these individuals. Whatever lessons they learn today, they shall put them into practice tomorrow. If their upbringing today is perfect, the society of tomorrow shall be awless. And if today's generation follows a faulty program of training it is imperative that tomorrow's society will be evil and perverted.

The personalities in the eld s of politics, education and society shall emerge from these elements. Today's children are tomorrow's parents. Today's children can be tomorrow's reformers. If they have received good training at the hands of their parents, they in turn can carry forward this practice with their children. If the parents have the will, they can be the instruments of the reform of the society for the future and with neglect of the children they can be the cause of the ruination of the society. By giving the right training to their children, the parents can render invaluable service to their society.

Education and training should not be treated as an insignicant subject. The efforts which the parents make to educate their children and the hardships that they undergo in this quest result in the creation of thousands of professors, doctors, and engineers. It is the parents who strive to nurture perfect human beings, capable and pious mentors and other professionals.

The mothers in particular bear more responsibility for the upbringing of the children. The children spend most of their childhood with the mothers. The foundation of the direction their future is bound to take is laid here. So, the key to the vice or virtue of a person and the progress or decline of a society is with the mothers of the society. The woman's place is not in the shop oor, ministerial or administrative positions. These functions don't measure up to the importance of a woman as a mother. Mothers breed perfect human beings. Virtuous ministers, lawyers, professors owe their positions to the loving care received from their mothers during their formative years.

The parents, who nurture truthful, pious children not only serve their children and the society but also create a niche for themselves in the society. These children will be a support of the parents in their frail old age. If parents strive towards the education and upbringing of their children they reap the harvest of their troubles during their lifetime only. 'Ali, The Commander of the Faithful, says:

"Evil off-spring is among the greatest hardships for the parents."(*Ghurar al hukm*, p. 189)

"Evil off-spring causes loss of respect for the parents and the successors are shamed." (*Ghurar al hukm*, p. 780)

The Prophet of Islam says:

"May Allah bless the parents who trained their children to behave justly with them." (*Makarim al akhlaq*, p. 517)

Therefore those who attain parenthood have great responsibility on their shoulders. This responsibility is to Allah Almighty as also to their fellow human beings and also to their own children. If they discharge the responsibility properly they will be rewarded in this world and hereafter.

But if they falter in the discharge of this responsibility then they themselves will be the losers and they will be tantamount to have cheated their own children and the society at large and they would be perpetrating an unpardonable sin.

The Knowledge and Mutual Cooperation of the Educators

The training and upbringing of a child is not an easy and simple task that the parents can perform with little or no effort. This task requires, in fact, delicate handling and temperament. There are myriads of ne points to be considered to achieve success in the efforts. The mentor has to relate himself with the spirit of the child. He cannot perform the task without knowing the spiritual, psychological, educational and practical niceties of the job.

A child's world is a world of his own and his imaginations and fantasies will be unique to him. These cannot be compared to the thought process of the adults. The child's spirit will be delicate and will be very impressionable. The child will be a human being in miniature that has not as yet assumed a permanent identity but it has the capability to attain this change.

The mentor of the child has to be capable of fathoming and identifying a human being and, also, identifying the mind of the children. He should have a keen eye on the intricacies of the process of upbringing. He should be aware of the human capabilities and failings. He should have sense of responsibility and keen interest in the job on hand. He should be patient and courageous that the hardships don't overpower him.

Besides, the rules of training are not rigid and cannot be implemented the same way under different circumstances. In fact these rules have to be modied and applied to each individual child according to his physical make up and mental capabilities. The parents must keenly observe the physical built of the child and educate him keeping this factor in mind. Otherwise, the effort may not bring about the desired result.

The man and woman should acquire knowledge about education and training before parenting a child. The education of the child commences with its birth and, in fact, from the time of conception. During this period the foundation of the child's nature is established and his nature, behavior, thinking process starts taking shape.

It is not right that the parents remain unconcerned during this visibly dormant period.

They postpone the upbringing of the expected new arrival till its actual arrival. They tend to keep away this task till the child is capable of distinguishing between good and bad behavior. While it may be easier to correct the behavioral defects in the early stages, it may be difcult, if not impossible, to effect these corrections once the habits are formed.

'Ali, The Commander of the Faithful, says:

"The most difcult politics is bringing about changes in the habits of people."[12] "Habits settle down upon people."[13]

"Habits become second nature."[14]

Shunning habits is so difcult that doing it is considered amongst

---

[12] Ghurar al Hukm, p. 181

[13] Ghurar al Hukm, p.580

[14] Ghurar al Hukm, p.260

better invocations. 'Ali, The Commander of the Faithful, says:
"Overcoming bad habits is amongst benevolent invocations."[15]

Another important factor in imparting ideal training to the child is the coordination and cooperation between the parents and other mentors like the grand parents on the program of training to be followed. Their joint effort will produce the desired results. But if any one of them takes a cavalier attitude on the training process, the results may not me as desired.

The child should be made aware of its duty. When the parents give contrary directions the child gets confused. Particularly if they insist on their contrary points of view, there is likelihood of negative results in the process of the training of the child.

The biggest difculty in imparting training to the child is that the father makes a decision about him and the mother or the grand parents insist on a contrary course. There is always a need for such understanding between the mentors that the child is able to clearly understand what he has to do and the idea of doing anything against this does not enter his mind.

Sometimes it happens that the father is well educated and reasonable and the mother of the child is ill tempered and uneducated. Sometimes the situation is reversed, when the mother is better equipped to train the child and the father is not. Many families face this problem. Children in such families do not receive proper training. But this doesn't mean that they should give up efforts of properly training their children.

In such a difcult situation the responsibility become more pronounced. The need in such a situation is to give more thought to the program of educating the child. The parents should make sincere efforts to overcome the lacunae in their character and behavior and

---

[15] Ghurar al Hukm, p.176

give more attention to the children.

With good actions the parents can attract the children's attention and set a desirable example before them. The parent's action should help the child to decide what is good for him and what is not. If the mentor is wise, thoughtful and patient he can to a greater extent counter the negative impact of his wife's behavior on the training of the child. This is no doubt a difcult task but there is no way out of it.

One intellectual says:

"A family in which the father and the mother think alike about the upbringing of the children and are able to mould their character and actions accordingly the impact on the senses of the children will be ideal.

The family unit is a small society in which the child's moral character assumes denite form.

A family in which the members are friendly towards each other their children are generally mild mannered, self respecting and judicious. Against this, a family where the parents have the habit of contradicting each other their children will be morally decient, pretentious and excitable."

Training Through Deeds, Not Just Talk

Most parents think that oral instructions and occasional talk about dos and don'ts is sufcient for good upbringing of children. They presume that the upbringing of the child is thus taken care of and they do not have to do anything about the upbringing of the child concerning other walks of life. This is why such parents do not feel any need to think of the upbringing till the child is a tiny tot.

They say that the child is still a babe and is incapable of understanding anything about upbringing. When the child comes to the age of understanding they give a thought to its upbringing. It is the period in the life of a child when he starts discriminating between good and bad. While this thinking is incorrect, the child, as a matter of fact, is ready for the upbringing the day he is born. He gets trained every moment and his nature is moulded in a particular way.

Whether the parents are aware of this process or not the child does waits not for any initiative on their part. The child's active mind and other senses are like a camera, which keeps preserving images of what happens in its environment. A child of ve to six years would have acquired a certain character. Good or bad habits would have got engrained in its nature and it would be a difcult task to bring about a change in his behavior.

The child, as a matter of fact, is a mimic. It tries to emulate its parents and the other inmates in its surroundings. The child views its parents with a degree of respect and makes efforts to copy their life style. Their actions become his yardstick for good and bad actions. The nature of a child is not cast in a mould but it takes the parents as the example to follow. The child depends more on the behavior of the parents as a model for its actions than any amount of sermonizing.

The daughter observes her mother and learns the niceties of house keeping. She sees her father and understands the nature of men. The boy takes lessons about life from his father's actions and from his mother's behavior he learns about the nature of women.

It is therefore necessary for responsible people to reform themselves at the outset and if they have any aws in their behavior they should avoid them. In a nutshell, they should mould themselves into good human beings before they embark on the road to parenthood.

The parents should give a thought to what sort of offspring the desire to give to the society. If they feel that their child should be a morally upright, kind, humane, freedom loving and responsible person then they too have to be owning such characteristics that they set an example for him to emulate.

The mother wishes that her daughter should be responsible, kind, equanimous person who respects the feelings of her spouse then she should herself try to t into these norms. The daughter will then observe the behavior pattern of the mother and automatically mould herself the same way. If the mother is an ill tempered, lazy, disorderly, untidy and selsh person then she cannot expect to train her daughter only through lecturing on the norms of good behavior.

Only those persons can competently train and bring up children properly who had similar upbringing themselves in their childhood.

They will have better understanding of the nature and psyche of the children. The parents who have differences and pick up ghts over trivialities will be incompetent in bringing up children. Similarly professional educators who have taken up the task only for the material remuneration, who are impatient, excitable and do not have an understanding of the child's nature and psyche will not be able to put their trainees on the right track.

Dr. Jalali writes:

"Whosoever has the responsibility of upbringing a child should occasionally do introspection on his own character and behavior, realize his responsibilities and try to correct his failings."

'Ali, The Commander of the Faithful, says:

"The person who is in the lead should rst reform himself and then try to correct others. Before teaching the norms of good behavior to others he should set an example himself. One who educates himself in learning and manners is more deserving of respect than he who only teaches the norms of good behavior to others."[16]

"You respect your elders that your children respect you."[17]

"If you wish to reform others, then commence the exercise with reforming yourself. If you like to correct others and keep yourself awed it will be the biggest blemish."[18]

"When the talking tongue is silent on sermonizing and the actions of the sermonizer speak for themselves, then no ears can keep the sermon out and nothing is more effectively benecial than this."[19]

One lady writes in a letter:

"…. my parents' character has deeply impressed me. They have

---

[16] As quoted in the edited work, Nahj al balaghah

[17] Ghurar al Hukm, p.546

[18] Ghurar al Hukm, p. 278

[19] Ghurar al Hukm, p.232

always been kind to their children. I never found any aw in their words or deeds. We also acquired this habit. I cannot forget their good character and behavior. Now that I am a mother my endeavor is to see that I don't do any thing in the presence of the children, which is not considered good. My parent's character is the example to be emulated in my life. I try to see that my children too are brought up the same way."

Another lady wrote in a letter:

"…. When I recapitulate my past life I recall that my mother used to argue and shout on trivial matters. Now that I am a mother I feel that with a little difference my condition is nearly the same as my mother's was. All her negative manners have become a part of my character. The strange problem is that however much I try to reform myself I am unable to make much progress. Denitely it is proved in my case that the parents' character and behavior has far reaching effect on the moulding of the character of their children. The saying, therefore, is correct that a mother with the good training of her children can transform the world."

Abstain from Domestic Differences

For a child the home is like a nest. He feels very much attached to it. His heart is always tied to it. If the parents are on friendly terms his nest remains durable like a warm lap. The child in such a home feels contented and secure. Getting an upbringing in such congenial atmosphere the latent qualities and capabilities in the child will truly nd expression and will bring out salutary results.

But if the parents are excitable and ghting type then the child will lose its calm and contentment and he will be uneasy and restless. The parents who argue and ght do not realize that the feelings of the poor child. In such a situation the children get frightened and with hurt hearts they seek some corner to hide themselves wondering as to why their parents are behaving in that manner.

Otherwise they seek the avenues of eeing from the nest that has been so dear to them and seek refuge in some lane or bazaar. The bitterest memories of a child are the times when the parents have heated, loud arguments and ghts. The children are unable to forget such scenes till late in their own lives.

These events remain etched on their psyche and have deleterious effect on their natures.

Such children have weak hearts and stunted physique. They will be heart broken and spend their lives miserably. It is quite possible that daughters of such parents carry an impression that all men are as harsh and rude as their own father is. This may lead to abhorrence of the very thought of marriage for such girls.

It is also possible that the sons of such homes think that all women are as ill mannered as their own mother is and decide to remain celibate all their lives. In such an environment the children become rebellious and start hating the parents and the things come to such a pass that some children become revengeful. The statistics indicate that lot of gallivanting, alcoholic and anti social children is the consequence of the disturbed atmosphere at home

If one thinks of the bitter events of his childhood when the parents had bitter differences then he will feel that despite the passage of long years the unpleasant memories are remaining etched on his mind.

One intellectual writes:

"The parents should know the fact that when there is an argument or ght between the elders of the house there will be deleterious effect on the thinking of the children. The type of relations the elders keep will have denite effect on development of the children….if the atmosphere of unity and peace is absent from the house then it is not possible to give proper upbringing to the children.

When the elders become argumentative and excitable they forget that the impressionable children are with them whose upbringing is their responsibility. In such an atmosphere the children do not learn any good lesson. The children then become secluded and ill tempered. Particularly children of slightly higher age nd the situation very difcult. Their hearts cry over the attitude of the father. They are unable to decide whose side they should take. In some cases they become antagonistic to both the parents."

Another person writes in a letter:

"….from the most unpleasant incidents of my childhood the vividly etched on my mind are those when my parents used to ght exchanging abusive language. During these events my sister my brother and myself used to stand shivering in a corner. As long as the ght continued we used to watch helplessly. I remember my sister used to cry at such events and these ts lasted for long. She is now a victim of nervous breakdown. It seems that the wrangles of our parents had a very bad effect on the spirit of my sister…."

Another person writes:

"…. the thought of an unpleasant event of my childhood doesn't leave my memory. My father was ill mannered, excitable and selsh. He used to invent excuses to ght at home and shout at everyone. Our parents used to ght throughout the day. I wonder they never tired of doing this. The ghts generally used to be on trivialities. There was no night when I went to bed without shedding tears. This was the reason that my nerves were weak. I am a scared person and I get bad dreams.

I have consulted doctors who say that the reason for my condition is the effects of the atmosphere at my home. He says that there is no cure for this other than rest and peace at home. My happy days started when I got married and I escaped from that house. Now, although my life is peaceful, I have a feeling that I am a defeated person and I cannot make much progress in life. I appeal to parents, In the name of God If you have any differences, do not ght in the presence of your children!"

He further writes in his long letter:

"The worst event of my life happened when I was eight years old. That day my parents had a very bad ght. All the children went scurrying to corners. The event had such a sad effect on my spirit that for a long time I couldn't erase the thought from my memory. I was fed up with my family and myself. I used to think that I should not return home from school. I used to offer a silent prayer to God that I die of some serious sickness.

Many a time I thought of committing suicide. Several times I dreamt that I was married and ghting with my spouse. During such dreams I used to plan a strategy for preserving my rights. After my marriage I tried several times to pick up a quarrel with my wife to demonstrate to her that I am an angry person.

Luckily my wife is of a cool nature. She treats me with love and affection and convinces me with good arguments and advice. It is my good luck that the ill temper did not last long with me. When I recall the mistakes of my parents I did introspection over my own failings and I tried hard to mend my nature. Now I am leading a peaceful life."

Another gentleman writes:

"…. When I was nine years old my parents separated because of acute differences. They left me, my sister and my brother in the care of our paternal grand father. We used to cry there very often. While visiting my mother I used to dream while sleeping that I wouldn't go to my father's house. After some time some well-meaning relatives intervened and made my parents to reunite.

My mother returned back to our home. But during that short break my spirit got so much affected that even now I feel sad about it. Now I make a serious effort that whenever I have any differences with my wife, we don't give vent to our feelings in the presence of our children."

Another letter reads thus:

"…. there are many bitter memories of my childhood and pleasant memories are but few. When I remember those days I become sad and I am unable to control the tears welling my eyes. The reason for this sadness is that I always found my parents arguing and ghting. Thus they made life difcult for us brothers and sisters. We are a family of eight children. I never argue with my husband that I do not become the cause of the bitterness of my husband and children."

In one letter someone writes:

"…. Age ve is the best part of one's childhood. When I was of this age there came about bitter differences between my parents. My father brought a second wife. Because of these differences my mother secured a divorce from my father. We were six brothers and sisters. One day turned very bitter for us. I was playing with one of my brothers when our mother came to say her adieus to us. God knows how sad we children were.

Our mother went away and we remained with our father and the new mother. We remained away from our own mother for two years bearing the pangs of negligence that our father showed to us. Then one day our mother came and took me and one of my brother's home. She had received some legacy from her mother's property.

With that inheritance she carried on our upkeep. Later on the other brothers and sisters too joined us. Our mother gave us the treatment of both a mother and a father. We cannot forget her courage and sacrices."

Another lady writes in her letter:

"…. my parents always used to quarrel and there was turmoil in our home. My mother always used to be angry. I was eight years of age when she used to leave my other siblings in my care and go out. My sister and brothers were of age two, four and six. I used to care for them to the best of my capability.

Sometimes I used to get beatings from our father.

Despite all the dificulty I was trying to continue my studies but I failed in my second standard. My tutors were aware of my dificulties. They took pity on me and gave me grace marks. In such circumstances I reached high school. Now I am also a mother. I make a sincere effort that differences do not plague me and my family."

The parents who feel their responsibility and they have interest in good upbringing of their children refrain from giving rise to any differences and ghts in the family and they denitely avoid airing any differences in front of the children. There is no worse act than the parents disturbing the children by squabbling in their presence and leaving them behind. If they realize the feelings of the children during such absences, however brief they are, then they would try never to ght again.

Such events are remembered till the end of one's life. However there are hardly any families where there is no meaningful difference of opinion. But in marital life there is always the need for rapprochement.

Wise and informed couples resolve their differences with cool and calm discussions.

If the children learn of the differences of their parents, they should handle the matter tactfully and convince them that the matter is being sorted out and they need not worry on that count. The parents should take care that they do not talk of divorce in the hearing distance of their children. This not only affects their married life but can cause damage to the delicate minds of the children.

Separation between husband and wife is a grave injustice to the children. They feel that their nest has fallen down. And their lives are shattered. This is naturally because the children have love for both the parents and cannot imagine any one of them abandoning them. If the children remain in the custody of the father after the divorce and he gets a second wife they will be required to unwillingly live under the care of a step mother.

However good and gentle the stepmother is, she cannot take the place of the real mother. General observation is that most stepmothers do not take good care for stepchildren. The newspapers carry many stories of bad treatment of children at the hands of stepmothers. If the children revert to the care of the separated mother, they still feel the void created by the absence of the father. And if the parents are so thoughtless that they leave the children to the care of foster parents, it will be very sad for the young kids.

Anyway, the husband and wife are free till they have children. But they have added responsibility after they have children and this will be the time when they have to make sincere efforts to avoid any serious differences cropping up. They must protect the good atmosphere at home and do not become the cause of worry to the children. Otherwise they will be answerable and subject to retribution in the Court of Allah.

Starting Life as a Mother

When the sperm of the man enters the womb of the woman and fuses with the ovum, the process of fertilization and the woman becoming a mother commences. The fertilized egg (the ovum) starts fast metamorphosis and ultimately takes the nal shape of a human being. In fact the age of a person can be counted from the day the process of fertilization takes place.

One intellectual writes:

"When a person arrives in this world, he would already have completed nine months of his age. And in these preliminary nine months he passes through a metamorphosis which determines the shape he gets ultimately as a complete human being for a complete lifetime."

When a woman is pregnant, she becomes a mother from that moment. She bears the responsibility for the child developing in her womb. It is a fact that the father's germ has a bearing on the legal inheritance, the physical and psychological make up of the person but the new arrival's future depends more on the care of the mother. The father's germ is like the seed but the development depends much on the developing environment it gets.

Another intellectual writes:

"The parents of a child can provide a growth environment which is ideal for its progress and can also give an environment which may be deleterious to its optimum development. If the growth environment is not proper it is not congenial for the immortal spirit of the off spring. This is the reason that the parents bear a heavy responsibility for the upbringing of the child."

Every person's welfare, illness, strength, weakness, looks, character take shape in the mother's womb. The rudiments of the child's morals and fate are established from the very womb of the mother.

The Holy Prophet says:

"The Fate, good or bad, of a person is determined when he is in the womb of the mother."[20]

The pregnancy is a very delicate period and puts tremendous responsibility on the expectant mother. A woman who is aware of her responsibility does not consider the pregnancy as an ordinary time and doesn't indulge in careless behavior. She knows that slight carelessness might affect her health badly and the baby she is carrying might get damaged. This damage could be so severe that the child arrives with irreparable defects that it may have to carry for the life.

Another intellectual writes:

"The mother's body and the events connected with it have an effect on the child she is carrying. The child in the mother's womb is very sensitive to the changes her body is undergoing. This is because the mother's body is complete and the child is developing to take the nal shape. Therefore it is the duty of every expectant mother to keep a good environment at the house.

She can succeed in this if she knows what events can have salutary effect on the child and what will not. A careful mother can provide

---

[20] Bihar al-anwar, v 77, p. 115

the right environment for the ideal development of the child in her womb.

An ideal environment for the child in pregnancy and immediately after birth is an utopia.

But the parents make their best effort to see that they provide an environment as near to perfect as possible. But the accidents of ignorance cannot be ruled out. If people are not aware of the consequences of carelessness, they may be faced with problems during pregnancy and after delivery of the child. One should realize that coming into the world without any physical defect is the right of every human being.

Welfare of the Embryo (Fetus) Depends on the Mother's Nutrition

In the womb of the mother the foetus is not an integral part of her body although it gets sustenance from her blood and nutrition. A pregnant mother's food has to be properly planned and balanced which has to provide nutrition not only for her maintenance but also to the foetus.

Therefore a pregnant woman's recipe of nutrition has to be meticulously planned. Otherwise there is always a risk that the deciency of certain vitamins and minerals in the food may prove deleterious to the health of the mother and the child.

In the eyes of Islam the nutrition of the pregnant woman is of prime importance to the extent that she can be exempted from mandatory fasting during the month of Ramadan. She is given the liberty to fulll her obligation after delivery of the baby.

Research proves that eighty percent of the genetically deformed children with physical and mental aberrations are because of decient food given to the mother during her pregnancy.[21]

---

[21] Aijaz e khurakiah, p.220

Dr. Jazairi, an eminent nutritionist, writes:

"It is known since long that the development of the foetus and the baby before birth and during feeding on mothers milk the nutrition received by the mother is very important. The mother has to take care that all the essential proteins, vitamins, carbohydrates, fats and other materials are taken in optimum quantities and at proper intervals for proper growth of the living cell that is the foetus. The foetus, which remains in the stage of metamorphosis in the womb, requires all these essentials for proper and healthy growth. It does happen during pregnancies that the mother remains healthy outwardly but due to deciency of certain vitamins the foetus shows abnormal growth."[22]

Karner says:

"Sometimes the reason for a new-born being abnormal is that although the seed is good it doesn't get a proper environment in the womb. It also is sometimes because although the womb's environment is good the seed is defective. In these conditions babies are born with several deformities like cleft lips, small and sunken eyes and at soles of the feet etc. Earlier these defects were thought to be genetic of nature but now the research points out that they are caused by decient availability of elements like oxygen during the pregnancy. The living environment and the surroundings during the pregnancy of a woman are considered the cause of the congenital defects like paraplegic limbs etc.

Imam as-Sadiq says in a tradition: "Whatever a pregnant mother eats or drinks, the foetus draws its sustenance from that."[23]

---

[22] Biography Before Delivery, p. 182

[23] Bihar al-anwar, v 6, p. 342

The Effect of the Mother's Nutrition on the Fetus

During pregnancy the type of food taken by the mother has a marked effect on the nature, intelligence and capability of the child. This is because the brain of the child responds to the quality of nutrition provided to the foetus by the mother during its growth. Islam has clearly dened that the mother's food intake during the pregnancy has a denite effect on the character of the child. Here some traditions on the subject are sited:

The Holy Prophet says:

"The mothers must ensure that during the nal phase of pregnancy they must eat dates that their children grow to be gentle and sober."[24]

"Ensure that your expectant wives eat behdana seeds (Seeds of Quince, a Central Asiatic tree of the rose family the fruit of which resembles a hard eshed yellow apple). Such wives bear children with good health and character."[25]

Imam Ridha' said:

---

[24] Mustadrak al-wasail, v 3, p. 113

[25] Mustadrak al-wasail, v 3, p. 116

"When pregnant women eat behdana seed it enhances intelligence and wisdom of the child."[26]

The prophet of Islam said: "The pregnant woman who eats melons will give birth to pretty and polite children."[27]

---

[26] Makarim al akhlaq, v 1, p. 196
[27] Mustadrak al-wasail, v 3, p. 635

The Mother's Nutrition

Research on the different types of food materials is not in the scope of this book nor can we enumerate the qualities of each because it is a subject that requires consideration at length. Nor is the author an expert on the subject of nutrition. Luckily many useful books have been published on the subject and the readers interested in a more detailed study may refer to such books. But it will not be out of place if we have a cursory look on the subject.

Although the nutrition intake requirement of pregnant women increases, it is a matter of worry that their appetite generally reduces in this condition. Many of them feel listless and dull. In such a state they need to plan to consume concentrates which are foods with lesser bulk and more nutritive value. The nutrients required by the human body are contained in different types of food materials. Therefore keeping variety in the ration of a pregnant woman gives scope for designing ideal feeding program for her.

The experts in this eld write:

"To keep the body t not only food intake is necessary but also it should be a planned mix of food materials taken at planned intervals."[28]

The mother should ensure that she takes supplemental vitamins and minerals with the morning and evening meals that will help the foetus in the seventh month. This will not only help in the proper growth of the teeth and the gums but also some other important bones of the body.[29]

Dr. Giasuddin Jazairi writes:

"Consumption of yoghurt and cheese during pregnancy provides vitamins and fats to the woman and prevents her from consuming many other unnecessary things which she might otherwise be inclined to eat. She should however avoid taking sour yoghurt. Stale cheese may also not taste well. At breakfast she should take a glass of milk and a broth of oats. Vitamin B is present plentifully in liver, kidneys, intestines that are useful foods and should form a part of the pregnant woman's diet.[30]

It is better that the pregnant women should take milk at regular intervals. This is a complete food and the Prophets in the past were very fond of this food.

Imam Ja'far as-Sadiq says:

"Milk is the food of the Prophets."[31] Dr. Giasuddin Jazairi writes:

"Most women feel pain in the limbs and the back due to deciency of calcium during pregnancy. They also nd their nails breaking during this period. They are therefore advised to consume fruits and vegetables that are rich in calcium. They have also to be particular to regularly take soup made from bones of sheep and lemon juice."[32]

---

[28] Ilm o zindagi, p 462

[29] Biography Pesh uz tawallud, p. 80

[30] Aijaz khurakia, p.223

[31] Bihar al-anwar

[32] Aijaz khurakia

Generally for people and in particular for the pregnant women the raw and cooked vegetables and fruits are considered good food. The plants derive the nutrients from the soil, water, air and sunlight and store the food for us. All the fruits have good nutritive value but particularly apples, quince, pears, dates are very useful.

Likewise every vegetable has its own nutritive value. Different vitamins and minerals are provided to the body by different food grains, fruits and vegetables. A person who wants to take good care of his nutrition should take a mix of fruits and vegetables and try to eat all the seasons fruits, even if occasionally. Particularly, the pregnant women should make a careful mix of different food materials in their diet. Islam exhorts its people and the pregnant womenfolk to eat fruits and vegetables. A few quotations are given here to prove our point:

Imam as-Sadiq says:

"Everything adorns some place or other and similarly the vegetables adorn the dining area."[33]

One day when Imam Ridha' sat for his meal he found the vegetable salad missing from the fare. He told to his servant, "You know that I don't eat food without the salads. Please bring the salads for me." When the salads were brought the Imam commenced his meal.

The Holy Prophet is on record saying,

"Eat quince because it enhances your intelligence, removes worries and makes the child gentle."[34]

The Prophet also said:

"Eat quinces and present its good fruits to your friends because it improves the eyesight and makes the hearts mellow. The pregnant women too draw lots of benet from this fruit and their new born

---

[33] Mustadrak al-wasail, v 3, p. 148

[34] Makarim al akhlaq, v 1, p. 196

children are pretty and healthy."[35]

"During the last months of pregnancy the women should eat the dates that their children have forbearing natures."[36]

'Ali, The Commander of the Faithful, says:
"Eat the dates that they are the cure of all pains."[37]

There are innumerable traditions of the Prophet and his Infallible Descendants that throw light on the high nutritive value of different fruits and vegetables. Nutritionists can devise ideal diet schedule including appropriate quantities of these fruits and vegetables for various requirements. Consulting a nutritionist or a specialist medical practitioner will be very useful.

---

[35] Makarim al akhlaq, v 2, p. 116

[36] Makarim al akhlaq, v 3, p. 113

[37] Makarim al akhlaq, v 3, p. 112

Consuming Tobacco

Pregnant women are advised to abstain from cigarettes and any other type of tobacco based product. Consuming of tobacco is not only deleterious to their personal health but will also have harmful effect on their foetus. In this connection we quote from a paper published in a foreign journal. We invite your attention to what it has to say:

"One study made in the Scandinavian countries on 6363 pregnant women showed that those of the group who smoke have given birth to babies on an average weighing 170 grams less than the babies of the women who do not smoke. This weight difference was recorded in 50% of pregnant women who habitually smoked. On the other hand the height of the babies of the smoker mothers was recorded to be less than the other group.

Similarly the heads and the bladders of the babies of smoker mothers were found to be smaller than those of non-smoker mothers are. The infantile mortality of the babies of the smoker mothers has also been recorded to be six times more than those from the other group. The children of the smoker mothers are likely to be born with physical defects than those of non-smoker mothers.

The use of cigarettes causes deciency of oxygen in the blood of the foetus thereby causing excessive production of hemoglobin. Congenital heart disease is 50% more prevalent in babies born to cigarette smoking mothers than others. Statistics prove that children of mothers who smoke are poorer at their studies when they go to school than those of the other group.

The intensity of this condition depends on the quantum of smoking the mother did during her pregnancy because the tobacco causes reduction in the cells of the brain of the foetus. What has been said above is only a part of the damage that can be caused to the baby of the mother who consumes tobacco.

Perhaps there are more serious damages caused by cigarette smoking that have not been identied so far. Therefore, all those mothers who are concerned about their own and their children's health should avoid smoking."[38]

Dr Jazairi writes:

"Tobacco smoking is harmful for the mother and also for the baby growing in her foetus. Alcoholic beverages too are very dangerous for carrying mothers. In addition to the poisonous effect of the alcohol it destroys the vitamins which are the essential requirement of the mother and her foetus. Such women have the risk of giving birth to babies with disabilities. Smoking and consumption of strongly brewed tea too are very harmful for pregnant women."[39]

Dr Jalali writes:

"Alcohol, marijuana and other drugs get into the blood stream of the parents and move into the embryo thereby affecting the growth of the foetus adversely. Some experts are of the opinion that when pregnant women smoke cigarette, the heart of the foetus is affected

---

[38] Maktab Islam, Year 15, Issue No. 6

[39] Aijaz khurakia, p.215

and its beats increase abnormally."[40]

---

[40] Rushinasi Kudak, p. 222

When Pregnant Women Fall Ill

When a pregnant woman needs medication for any indisposition, she has to exercise utmost care in the consumption of medicines because the medicines are generally designed for adults and might not be compatible for the delicate foetus and affect it adversely. It cannot be predicted what effect the drugs might have on the foetus. It is a fact there is no medicine, which will not affect the foetus. This is the reason a pregnant mother must exercise maximum restraint in taking medicines.

Firstly, she should avoid intake of medicine. But if the condition of the health becomes such that medication becomes absolutely necessary, then she should have access to it on the expert advice of a medical practitioner who can suggest the right medicine and the dosage.

When the illness is risky for the mother and the child, the pregnant mother should obtain expert medical opinion and treatment, as, otherwise it might cause irreparable damage to the foetus.

One expert writes:

"It is possible that certain viruses and microbes escape from the mother and the father into the indefensible foetus and infect it with the same disease which the parents were suffering from."

He writes at another place:

"Any change in the dietary habit of the mother, the medicines which she has to take and the diseases with which she gets aficted will have effect on the embryo. Any diseased condition, which affects the embryo in the initial stages of conception, will progressively enhance. It is therefore imperative that the pregnant women should prevent themselves against diseases. Sometimes diseases may destroy their capacity to conceive in the future.

He also writes:

"There are several non-food materials which, when consumed by a pregnant mother, will adversely effect the development of the foetus. Most of the medicines are for adults and their trials are made only on grownups before they are approved for prescription. The viruses, bacteria and the germs in the body of the mother sometimes affect the foetus too.

Sometimes the foetus starts getting the same symptoms of the disease or sometimes abnormal growth takes place in the foetus because of the infection."[41]

---

[41] Biography Pish az tawalud, p. 182

Effect of the Psychological Condition of the Mother on the Embryo

The experts have been deliberating the fact whether the psychological condition of the mother has any effect on the embryo she is nursing.

Some experts say that if a mother is confronted with excessive fear and unease then the foetus will get affected and there is a strong possibility that the child will be timid and also the tendency of jealousy and malicious nature of the mother will be there in the child. As against this the good nature, humanity, honesty, boldness and affection in the mother will have a salutary effect on the nature of the offspring.

These experts are of the opinion that the child in the womb of the mother is in fact a part of her and therefore it will be inuenced by the thoughts and psyche of the mother. But there are some geneticists and child psychologists who reject this theory. They feel that it is not necessary that the psychological condition and thoughts of the mother inuence the mind of the newborn permanently.

Dr Jalali writes:

"There is no direct contact between the mother and the foetus but it is only through the umbilicus which does not possess any senses and the closed umbilicus has blood carrying nerves, therefore the earlier opinion that the psychological condition of the mother inuences the mind of the child may not be correct."⁴²

But, the truth is with the intellectual, that it cannot be claimed that the thoughts and psychological condition of the mother indirectly inuences the mindset of the child. But it is not right to say that the mother's thoughts have no direct effect at all on the mind of the child. This point of view is illustrated in the following arguments:

1. The human mind and spirit are connected to each other. The illness and good health of the human body and the strength of the nerves and physical potential or weakness and even the appetite or lack of it has a bearing on the thinking and morals of the person. The moral personality of an individual and his nature have a bearing on the development of his brain It is possible that the deciency or absence of food might give rise to the nervousness and amoral thoughts in the brain.
2. The embryo utilizes the food, which gets synthesized in the womb of the mother and reaches it. As long as the child remains in the mother's womb it depends on her for its sustenance. The mother's food habits therefore have a direct bearing on the physical and mental development of the child.

Dr Jalali writes:

Whatever is benecial for the mother is also benecial for the foetus. If the mother's food is decient in calcium, this deciency will affect the development of the bones and the teeth of the child.⁴³

---

[42] Rowan shinashi kudak, p. 188

[43] Rowan shinashi kudak, p. 188

1. This is well known that extreme disturbance and restlessness in a person causes indigestion, constipation and affects his body. Excess of sadness or fear reduces the appetite of a person and his digestive system gets impaired. The digestive glands do not function normally.

In the light of the above three points it can be said that although the mother's thoughts and spiritual condition do not directly transfer to the brain and nerves of the child, it is related to her digestive function which can ultimately affect the child's physical and spiritual make-up.

The mother's pangs of anger or uneasiness will affect her general nature and disturb her digestive system. This condition is damaging to the mother's body as also to the foetus.

It is possible that the child in such a mother's womb gets aficted with such disease, which might manifest itself at a later stage.

Dr Jalali writes:

"The pangs of excessive uneasiness suffered by the pregnant mother and the unpleasant happenings in her environment are denitely harmful to the development and the nature of the child. Such conditions create problems and give rise to the unwanted glands. Because of this the digestive system is unable to perform its normal function. Perhaps this is the reason that some children have several nervous ailments. These conditions may also be responsible for the miscarriage of the foetus."[44]

A pregnant lady physically and mentally at ease will have her foetus in good health. Such peaceful environment is ideal for the perfect development of the child in its mother's womb. To the contrary the foetus of a jealous, envious, excitable, timid and mentally ill mother will not be properly nurtured and can be affected with several ailments

---

[44] Rowan shinashi kudak, p. 222

of mind and body.

In this regard:

"The psychological experts have proved that 26% of psychologically ill children have inherited the condition from their mothers. Therefore if a mother is hale and hearty then her child too shall be the possessor of good physical condition. If the mother cares that her child is healthy then she should take good care of her own physical and mental well being during the pregnancy. The effects of the environment on the development of the child are always pronounced."

An Advice to Pregnant Women

Pregnant women are advised to abstain from lifting heavy materials. They should also avoid very tiring tasks. If a carrying mother tires herself, she is likely to tire the baby too. In such cases there is the danger of miscarriage of the pregnancy.

Travelling during the last months of pregnancy too is not advised. If there is no urgent need of travelling, it is better the carrying mothers do not undertake a journey in that period. However doing light work and restricted movement is not harmful and, in fact, is benecial for the health of both the mother and the child.

Dr Jalali writes:

"Excessive fatigue in pregnant women gives rise to poisonous substances in the blood. Since this blood is the source of nutrition for the foetus, it can adversely affect the growth of the child."[45]

---

[45] Rowan shinashi kudak, p. 222

Clean Enviornment

The growing child in the mother's womb requires oxygen although the foetus cannot breathe itself. But it utilises the oxygen acquired by the mother from the atmosphere. The mother not only consumes oxygen for her own sustenance but also provides it to the foetus. If the mother breathes in a clean and hygienic atmosphere she can ensure her own health and that of the child she is bearing.

If the mother's environs are polluted and she is breathing poisonous air, then there will be danger of illness aficting her and the child. The pregnant women are therefore advised to take particular care of the environment in which they live. They should move in pollution free environment and breathe deeply. The pregnant women should also avoid late nights, which might tire them excessively.

During pregnancy the women should avoid smoking and protect themselves from breathing in any polluted environment. While sleeping they should keep the windows of the bed-room open so that fresh breeze is available to them. It must be noted that deciency of oxygen might be very harmful to the foetus.

We are repeating the following paragraph from Dr Jalali, which has also appeared earlier in this book, for your attention:

"Various defects in the body like cleft lips, at soles of the feet, sunken and small eyes were previously thought to be of genetic reasons. But now it has been found that these defects in the new born children are because of the environmental conditions and particularly the deciency of oxygen during the pregnancy of the women."

Miscarriage

There is no objection in Islam to contraception or family planning with the mutual consent of the spouses. If the wife and the husband desire not to have any more issues, they can prevent conception with harmless pills, injections and other contraceptive methods. But obviating birth of already conceived is undesirable in Islam. Islam wants that the progeny of its followers ourish. When the male and female cells have fused to form an embryo, it is the rudiment of a living being and its abortion is forbidden in Islam.

Although the embryo is a minuscule object, it has full right to existence. It is an existence, which is fast developing towards becoming a full-edged human being. This small creature wants its mother to provide congenial environment to grow in and take birth as full-edged human. If one aborts such an existence, one has committed murder and the act will be liable to punishment of the parents on the Day of Judgment.

The Faith of Islam, which is the guardian of the rights of all, has banned completely the abortion and infanticide. Ishaq bin Ammar says, "I submitted to Imam Mua ibn Ja'far that in case a woman is scared of getting pregnant do you permit her to take medicine which brings about abortion. The Imam replied, "No I cannot give such a permission!".

The narrator again said, "What is the decree for the time when the pregnancy is in its initial embryonic stage?"

The Imam replied, "The development of man commences with the formation of the embryo. Allah says in the The Holy Qur'an,

> *"On the Day of Judgment the parents will be asked: for what crime you have killed your innocent child?"* *(The Holy Qur'an, 81:8-9)*

Abortion of foetus is a very amoral act, which Islam has forbidden. Also, such operations are highly risky for the life and health of the mother. Dr Pak Nagar, addressing a seminar on abortion has said"

".... it has been proved that forcing abortions reduces the expected age of the woman. Scientic research also has proved that abortion upsets the psychological balance of the woman's mind."[46]

From 1951 to 1953, according to the statistics of the New York City, 2601 women died during abortions. In the next ten years the fatality on this account has risen by 42%. In Chile 39% of female deaths were on account of abortions.

One excuse for having access to forced abortions is poverty. Some parents take shelter behind their poverty to kill their innocent children.

There is no doubt that lots of families are victims of poverty. It is no doubt very difcult to bring up a family in the midst of poverty. But Islam does not accept the excuse of aborting children because of the unfortunate condition of poverty and penury. Allah says in the Holy

---

[46] Maktab e Islam, Year 13, Issue 8

The Holy Qur'an:

"Do not kill your children with fear of poverty. We give you and them the sustenance. Killing children is denitely a big sin." (The Holy Qur'an, 17:31)

When the foetus has already formed, the parents should bear the hardship courageously that possibly the child might grow into a great person and bring laurels for the family and the society. Possibly the child may become the cause of the economic well being of the family and they get relief from their poverty.

Other excuses are also made for undergoing abortions like outdoor activities, ofcial responsibilities and already having too many children. But these are not such valid excuses that the Islamic Jurisprudence and common sense permit abortions.

Not only abortion is unlawful in the eyes of Islam but also retribution has been xed for this sinful act which differs according to the age of the foetus which has been aborted forcibly.

Imam as-Sadiq says:

"If the aborted child is in embryo form then the blood money is equal to 20 dinars of gold. If the pregnancy has reached the form of a lump of esh, the blood money has to be forty dinars of gold. If the pregnancy has advanced to the form of muzga and esh the blood money has to be sixty gold dinars and if the foetus has formed bones the levy is eighty gold dinars. If the foetus has reached total human form the levy is one hundred gold dinars. If the aborted child is so developed that it has spirit in it, then the deet or punishment will be one human life.[47]

The lady, Afsar al Maluk Amili has written a beautiful poem on this

---

[47] Wasail al-shia, v 19, p. 169

subject, translated as under "The tiny aborted child appeared in my dream and said:

'If you meet my mother, ask her, mother:
What fault you found in me that you shed my blood unnecessarily!
As a child I was biding my time peacefully, then why the order for my killing?!
You have sharpened your fangs and paws, and have sullied your lapel with my blood! I was a newly arrived guest with you and had caused no harm to you.
Guests are there to be entertained, not to be killed heartlessly
You were worrying about the expenses for my upkeep that you extinguished my tiny existence! Mother! I had brought my sustenance with me, but it is a pity you didn't believe in it!
You preferred to keep yourself free to move around, instead of looking after me, and laid the foundation for tyranny!
For children the mother is their hope and with her they are contented!
I wished that I look at your face and pick owers from your beauteous garden. I wished to suckle milk from your bosom and thus relieve your sorrows.
I wished that I drank your milk and your voice reached my ears
I thought that when you saw my smiles you would sit near me on my bed.
I hoped that you would send me to school and give me the lesson of righteousness. Returning home from school I would make you happy by reciting the nursery rhymes. I wished that when I am a youth, then you would realize my value.
In your frail old age I would have been your prop and help.
Now I am in the Heaven like a pure spirit and my place is with the houris.
You should now express repentance that perhaps the Merciful Allah forgives you. O Afsar My request to you is to is to convey my message to all the mothers'

Difficult Deliveries

Pregnancy generally lasts for nine months and ten days. The pregnancy period is very sensitive and full of risks because it has a bearing on the future of the growing foetus. The child in the period spends its life within that enclosure over which it has no control and can be exposed to several physical and psychological dangers.

The child will not have capabilities of himself confronting and contending with these risks. After completing the nine months in the womb successfully it has to pass through another risky phase which is delivery. The process of delivery is not easy and simple but it is very sensitive and difcult.

The child grows to a size in the nine months that particularly its head at this stage is much larger than other parts of the body that its delivery from the narrow passage of the womb becomes very difcult. The possibility during delivery is always there that the child's bones get crushed or twisted. There can also be the likelihood of the brain getting damaged due to the pressure during parturition.

One expert writes:

"The process of delivery can possibly cause psychological defects in the child. Psychiatrists are of opinion that the process of delivery of a child will have a signicant bearing on its entire life. In their view delivery is a revolutionary change in the environment and life of the child and deprives it of the security and rest, which it had so far in the foetus. At the time of delivery fear and concern becomes a part of the psyche of the person. The future life of the person is spent imagining unknown thoughts of troubles. The life spent in the foetus was carefree and delivery is the arrival in the travails of the world."[48]

Dr. Jalali writes:

When a child arrives in the world, it will be under pressure for a few hours and the most affected will be its head that will be the largest part of the body at birth. If the delivery is not normal then the arrival will be more difcult and besides the risk of the environment, the child has to face the risks of handling with mechanical instruments used during the delivery. In such cases there is chance of infantile mortality. The illnesses like madness and paralysis in children may also me related to difcult deliveries.[49]

Therefore, delivery of children is not a simple process and requires utmost care and skill to ensure safety of the mother and the child. A little carelessness on the part of the handlers might cause great damage to the mother and the child, sometimes resulting in mortality of either or both. But nowadays the facilities of skilled doctors and specialty medicines are in the access of people and the likelihood of harm to the mother or the child is much reduced.

The pregnant ladies are advised that if they have access to a good gynecologist or a nursing home, they should consult them much ahead of the delivery. They must ascertain from the doctor the expected date of delivery and seek admission to the nursing home ahead of the

---

[48] Biography Pish az tawallud, p. 160

[49] Ruwan shinashi kudak, p. 193

delivery that they get better care than they can at home.

The main advantage in such cases is that the doctors and nurses are available at the nursing homes and if there is any emergency it can be attended to without much loss of time. If, while staying at home, a pregnant woman faces an emergency, the delay in reaching her to the doctors might result in danger to the mother and the child.

The other valid reason for sending the pregnant woman to the maternity home prior to the delivery is that the same sanitary environment and personalized medical attention cannot be provided at her own home.

Another advantage of going to the maternity home is that the chances of the pregnant lady facing unnecessary and unwarranted interference and opinions of the other women from the family will not be there. Generally such opinions are not educated and they may at times be harmful.

The husband too has a big responsibility during the pregnancy and delivery of his wife. Religiously and morally it is his duty that during this delicate and hazardous time he should provide help and courage to the wife and take all the possible steps to ensure safe delivery of the child.

Carelessness on the part of the husband may even sometimes result in the loss of the mother and the child or they sustain physical and psychological damage. Such heedless husbands will be deemed criminal in the eyes of religion and the society and they will be answerable on the Day of Judgment.

They will also suffer the pangs of remorse if for reasons of carelessness or miserliness they avoid providing necessary care to the pregnant wives.

Sometimes, because of the neglect at the required time the husbands have to incur much more expense to salvage the resultant damage. If the families of the pregnant women do not have access to the maternity homes then they should take the services of the competent midwives who have necessary skills and experience of attending to deliveries. In this regard the following precautions must be taken:

1. The temperature of the labor room should be moderate and it should not be too cold. This is important because the pregnant women will be under tremendous pressure and due to the long hours of labor pain they will be indisposed and sweating and there can be likelihood of the babies catching colds and getting exposed to several ailments. If the delivery room becomes colder after the delivery the mother will most likely catch cold. The cold wind is very harmful for the new born baby because the environment in the mother's womb will be warmer (having the normal human temperature (37.5 degrees Centigrade) and the room temperature will be much less. The body of the baby at the delivery will not have sufcient strength to adjust to the change Such babies are likely to fall ill and their treatment is rather difcult. Mortality rate in such babies is rather high.
2. It is necessary to prevent the air in the delivery room from becoming poisonous with the smoke of burning kerosene oil or coal. Breathing such polluted air is dangerous for both mothers and children.
3. It is advisable to maintain privacy in the delivery rooms to the extent possible. Keep unnecessary visitors out of the labor room. Such visitors might cause embarrassment and unease to the pregnant woman and may carry infections when they come from outside. Other women looking at the private parts of a woman is prohibited under Islam. During deliveries the pregnant women will be unable to cover their private parts. Imam Sajjad ordered other women to leave the labor room when a pregnant woman

was delivering lest her private parts are exposed to them.[50]

A responsible pregnant woman should exercise all care during pregnancy and delivery that she delivers a healthy baby to the society that it becomes a useful member of the community. In the view of Allah too it is the best service that a woman can give and will get its reward. One day the Prophet was speaking on the subject of Jihad.

One lady asked, "O, Prophet of Allah Will the women be deprived of the benets of Jihad?" The Prophet replied that the woman too gets the benet of the Jihad that the time from the conception to delivery and feeding of the child till its weaning the woman is like the man who is at the battleeld doing Jihad. If that woman dies during this period she would have achieved martyrdom."[51]

---

[50] Wasail al-shia, v 10, p. 119

[51] Makarim al-akhlaq, v 1, p. 268

After the Birth

When a child takes birth the air gets into its lungs and it starts breathing. After commencing the act of breathing the baby cries for the rst time. This crying is because of the reaction of the air getting into the lungs. If the child doesn't breathe and cry, it is held with its feet up and the head is gently stroked to help it breathe.

Then the umbilicus is tied and is severed with a sanitized scissors. After this the child is given a bath with soap and lukewarm water and clothed. For sometime the child does not need feeding. Then drops of warmish water mixed with sugar are put into the child's mouth.

The newborn will generally be in a state of dreaming. It needs lot of rest because it has undergone external and internal transition. Earlier it was dependent on the mother's nutrition but now its own digestive system has to start functioning.

During pregnancy the child depended for oxygen on the mother's breathing but after delivery its own respiratory system has to start functioning. It now takes its own oxygen from the atmosphere and ejects carbon dioxide during breathing. Its internal functioning would have undergone a major change and its external condition and environment is also totally changed. Earlier in the womb of the mother the temperature was 37.5 Degrees Centigrade but now it is in an environment which has transient temperature conditions.

During delivery too the child is subject to lot of pressure which needs mitigation. At this time the child will be like a postoperative patient who has just come out of an operation theatre who, above all, needs lots of rest. It will be like a machine, which has just come out of the shop oor, which needs delicate and careful handling. In this circumstance the best that can be done for the child is to provide him restful environment that it overcomes the hardship faced during the process of delivery.

Dr Jalali writes:

"Tickling the child to laughter, lifting it up repeatedly, changing its garments frequently and showing it to others are not desirable acts, which one should refrain from. The child is not a toy and it needs rest and peace. Avoid speaking loudly in its presence and refrain from lifting him up and down in an attempt to soothe him. Hugging and kissing the child too are not good for him."[52]

The mother too needs lots of rest and strength. During the nine months of pregnancy she would have gone through lots of travails. Especially after delivery she would be very weak as if she has lost most of the blood from her body. At this time the thoughtful husband: should provide to her all possible comforts and with good nutrition try to put her back to normal health. If medical attention and medication is required, then it should be provided without any loss of time. If the husband is negligent at this juncture then the wife will remain dull and weak and the consequences will have to be borne by him too.

---

[52] Ruwan shinashi kudak, p. 223

Mother's Milk - The Best Nutrition

The mother's milk is the best and complete food for the child. In many ways it can be preferred over the other food products available for them, like: the milk of cow, goat or commercially branded milk foods.

1. The mother's milk, on account of its nutrient value, will be ideally suited for the machinery of the child. It is very compatible for the child's needs because it has been drawing nutrition from the mother for nine months during the pregnancy and will continue to get the same contents from the milk provided by the mother.
2. Because the mother's milk is utilized in its natural condition it retains its nutritive value. To the contrary the cow's milk has to be boiled before use and many nutrients might get destroyed in the process.
3. From the point of view of the child's health the mother's milk is most preferable because it is least likely to be contaminated with germs because it is fed to child directly from the bosom. The other milk passes through many utensils and can be infected by germs in the process.

4. The mother's milk is always consumed fresh, while the other milk might spoil during storage.
5. There is no likelihood of adulteration of mother's milk but other milks have that risk.
6. Mother's milk will be free of disease causing germs but other milk has the risk of carrying such organisms.

Mother's milk is the safest food for the newborn and other babies. The children brought up on the mother's milk are healthier as compared to those who are fed on milk from other sources. Infant mortality in children fed on mother's milk is also found lesser than in the case of the other group.

There is another advantage in the mother feeding the child on her own milk is that her periods are delayed and the chances of her getting pregnant again are postponed to that extent.

Islam too stresses the importance of the mother's milk for the child and terms it the natural right of the child to be fed on it.

'Ali, The Commander of the Faithful, says:

"No other milk is as good as the mother's milk for the child."[53]

The mother's milk is of such prime importance in the eyes of Islam that when she feeds her child on it, she is earning rewards for the Hereafter.

The Prophet of Islam has said:

"As many times as a mother suckles her milk to the child, so many times Allah's reward to her will be equivalent to freeing a slave from the tribe of Ismail. When she reached the weaning stage, an Angel would put his hand on the arm of the mother and say,' start your life afresh that your past sins have been pardoned!'"[54]

---

[53] Wasail al-shia, v 15, p. 175

[54] Wasail al-shia, v 15, p. 175

At a seminar in the University of Shiraz the experts agreed, to the last person, that any other food or combination of vitamins cannot be a substitute of the mother's milk for the newborn child.

Dr Simeen Waki says:

"It is a matter of concern that lots of mothers, blindly following the practice of the Western women, forcing early weaning on their children, give them dehydrated milk powders and other synthetic baby foods. This practice is against the nutritional requirement of the child and is no substitute for the mother's own milk which is superior in every respect."[55]

Another expert writes:

"The mother's milk is a unique food which nature has provided for the babies and no other feed is substitute for that. Therefore every effort should be made to see that the mother is able to feed the baby on her own milk. If the mother is running dry, she should take extra care of her own nutrition to revive lactation."[56]

The responsible and informed mothers who are interested in the welfare of their children don't deprive them of the bounty that Allah has provided to them. These women know the effect of the milk on the body and mind of the growing child. Therefore they sacrice their own comfort for the health and welfare of the child. Only such women deserve to be called mothers and not those ignorant and selsh women who, despite proper lactation, render themselves dry and bring up the children on dried milk powder.

The women who do not feed their babies on their own milk might become victims of several physical and psychological ailments. The cancer of the breast is one serious ailment that is prevalent in such women.

---

[55] Behdasht jismi rawa kudak, p. 63

[56] Aijaz khurakia, 258

It is appropriate here to draw the attention of the mothers who feed babies on their own milk to take special care of their personal diet. The nutrition that the mother takes has a direct bearing on the nutritive value of the milk she produces. The mother's food should be a balanced combination of different fruits, vegetables and grains.

Fluid and succulent foods are useful. The mothers should not think that only expensive food could be good food. They can judiciously plan a balanced food that can be nutritious and not expensive at the same time. They can refer to good books on diet planning for this purpose. One such books observes:

"Expert dieticians advise that lactating mothers should consume a combination of food products available to them. In particular they should include lubia beans, grams, milk, fresh butter, coconut, olives, walnuts, almonds, sweet and succulent fruits like water melon, gurma or musk melon, and pears etc."[57]

Imam as-Sadiq says:

"If you have engaged a Jewish or Christian woman to foster feed your child then ask her to abstain from consuming pork and alcoholic beverages."[58]

If the feeding mother falls ill and has to take medication, she must keep the matter in mind that her own milk might get the effect of the medicines and harm the child who feeds on it. The mother should not indulge in using medicines without consulting a competent medical doctor.

---

[57] Aijaz khurakia, 251-256

[58] Mustadrak al-wasail, v 2, p. 224

Supplement the Mother's Milk

The principal food of the baby is no doubt the mother's milk but it is better to supplement judiciously with a little sh oil and fruit extracts. This will ensure that the feed is complete and the child grows in a better way. As the child grows its requirement of food increases. It reaches a stage when the mother's milk becomes insufcient for the child.

At this stage other food materials are included in the child's diet to provide optimum level of nutrition. After four months of delivery, or latest by six months, the child must be trained to eat other foods. It is important that the baby's feed is soft and succulent. Juices of different fruit can be ideal at this stage.

Water strained after boiling vegetables in it can be a good source of nutrients for the child. Soups are good for the growth of the child. When the child starts setting teeth the diet can have boiled potatoes, boiled eggs, biscuits, fresh cheese, bread, butter and fresh fruits. There should be variety in the diet of a child, but care has to be taken that it is not over fed.

Weaning from Mother's Milk

There are certain times when a child is deprived of the mother's milk.

1. The time when the mother is affected with some infectious disease.
2. When the mother is suffering from a serious health condition like a heart attack and the doctors advised not to breast-feed the baby.
3. When the mother is mentally ill or suffers from epilepsy.
4. When the mother is suffering from anemia and feeding the baby on her own milk may be harmful to both.
5. When the mother is addicted to drugs and alcoholic beverages because her milk poisoned by these materials will harm the baby.

In such conditions when there is the danger of infecting the baby or transferring poisonous matter through the milk, it is better to avoid feeding on the mother's milk. When the breast-feeding mother becomes pregnant, she should wean the child in stages and simultaneously introduce other foods in the diet.

The Schedule of Breast Feeding

The experts have suggested two methods for feeding of the babies. Some are of opinion that for feeding the child well thought out schedules have to be devised and the feeding should be done implicitly at those predetermined intervals. Between two feedings some have prescribed a delay of three hours and some suggest a gap of four hours. In the interim period it is recommended to abstain from feeding the baby.

Some other experts do not approve of this type of scheduling. And they believe in feeding the baby more frequently on the basis of the indication of the appetite by the baby. They say that whenever the baby shows the desire for food, it must be fed.

Some other nutritionists feel that the latter method of feeding is more suitable as they believe that the baby must get the milk whenever it shows signs of hunger. Both the methods, however, have their own pros and cons as illustrated here:

1. Hunger or thirst of a child cannot be determined positively because it cannot express its need clearly. In the initial stage of feeding it will be drinking the milk for sating its appetite and

then it continues to suckle the breasts. In such situations the child cries not so much with hunger as with the desire to suckle the mother's breast.

The mother too gives her milk to the child to stop his crying. Often the child cries without any appetite for food but the mother gives it the milk thinking that it is hungry. The child therefore drinks the mother's milk while it has the appetite and sometimes when it doesn't. It is a well established fact that taking of food at erratic intervals is not good for the health of the children as it is for the adults this habit might upset the digestive system of the child.

This is why unplanned feeding of babies is fraught with risk of illness for them. 'Ali, The Commander of the Faithful, says:

"Excessive eating and eating more thereafter should be avoided. Those who eat more are more likely to fall ill."[59]

1. The child who drinks milk without any controlled schedule will have a disorganized existence from the very beginning and grow into a disorderly adult.
2. It is common practice that whenever a baby cries, the mother's breast is given to it without trying to determine the cause of the crying. Such children get into the habit of skulking all the time. They think that crying and shouting is the only way to get things done according to their wishes. They can never show patience and courage in doing anything. They want to achieve their end immediately even if they have to cry profusely for the purpose. They do not feel ashamed at playing such shameful antics.
3. The parents and other members of the families are always restless because of such children.

---

[59] Mustdarak al-wasail, v3, p. 82

Dr Jalali writes about such children:

"If the feeding schedule of a child is xed in consultation with an expert pediatrician then it will get used to the timings and the mothers will understand when the child is hungry and when its appetite is sated.

Secondly, people do their daily tasks as a force of habit. Similarly feeding of the child too becomes a habit and is done almost automatically at the scheduled timings.[60]

Russel says:

"These days an ordinary mother knows the norms of bringing up children. She knows that it is important to feed the baby at predetermined intervals and not whenever it cries for some reason or the other. She knows that such regime is followed to keep the digestive system of the baby in good trim…

When the children see that the parents are acceding to their cries, it becomes their second habit and keeps crying at the slightest excuse. It also happens that the repeated episodes of crying over a long period earn them the anger of their parents. When the children realize this, they become morose and the world looks cold, dry and bleak to them."[61]

Attention must be paid to a few points:

1. For all the children the same program of feeding could not be possibly adopted. Every child will have its own digestive and nutritive requirements. And also the food requirements of any child are very dynamic. The digestive system of the new-born will be delicately tiny for the rst forty to fty days from birth. Therefore it can retain very small quantity of milk. It will be able to take a very small quantity of milk at a time. But it becomes

---

[60] Ruwan shinasi kudak, p. 224

[61] Dar Tarbiat, p. 78

The Schedule of Breast Feeding

hungry very soon thereafter. During this period the feeding times have to be of shorter intervals, say, every hour and a half to two hours. But as the children grow the gap between the feeds have to be increase, say, a feed every three to four hours or even more.

2. All the children will not be of the same physical condition and digestive capacity. Therefore an individual feeding program has to be developed for every individual child. Some children become hungry quite soon after a feed and others take more time for the same. Careful mothers are very observant and they take care to design an ideal schedule of feeding for their children in consultation with experts.
3. Whenever milk is given to the baby, care has to be taken that it is fully satised with the feed. But mothers must carefully observe that the newborn babies fall asleep while feeding on their breasts. In such instances they may not be fully fed and the mother has to gently strike the back of the child that it wakes up and completes its feed.
4. When the complete program of feeding the child is prepared it must be put to practice very carefully. The gaps between the feeds must be strictly adhered to. In between two scheduled feeds the child must not be given the milk even if it cries. This task needs patience and rmness on the part of the mother to ensure that the child gets used to the regime. Then the child will awake automatically at the scheduled time to receive its feed. Patience and forbearance will become a part of the nature of such children.
5. The feeding schedule of the children must be prepared in such a way that from midnight to dawn there is no need of feeding it. When the child takes to this habit, both the mother and the child will have a good night's rest.
6. The breasts must be cleaned with a little cotton wool after every feed. This is essential for the health and hygiene and will also

prevent the chance of injury to the breast.

7. When a child suckles the mother's milk some air too enters its digestive tract and makes it uneasy. Therefore, after every feed the child has to be raised a little and its back is gently tapped to see that the air comes out of its digestive system.

8. The suckling baby should be fed from both the breasts of the mother. This should be done to avoid drying of the milk, which can result in the pain of the breast. One lady says, "Imam as-Sadiq told to me, 'do not feed your child only from one of your breasts to ensure that it gets complete food.'"[62]

9. The lactating mothers should take care that they do not perform very tiring physical tasks and avoid spells of anger. This is advised because such events can affect their capacity to produce milk, which ultimately is bad for the child.

---

[62] Wasail al-shiah, v15, p. 176

If the Mother is Deficient in Milk

I f the mother is unable to satisfy the appetite of the baby, she has no right to deprive the baby of her own milk. She must breast feed the baby to the extent of the milk available with her and supplement it with other milk and nutrition. But if the mother is totally dry, which condition is quite rare, she can wean the child and turn to the cow's milk, which is qualitatively very similar to the mother's milk. When shifting to the cow's milk the following have to be borne in mind:

1. The cow's milk is generally denser and heavier than the mother's milk. Therefore it should be diluted with some boiled water before feeding to the child so that it comes closer to the density of the mother's milk. The milk should also be sweetened with a little sugar.
2. The cow's milk should be boiled for fteen minutes to ensure that any germs present there are destroyed.
3. The milk, while feeding to the baby, should neither be too hot nor very cold. The temperature of the milk to be ideally close to the temperature of the mother's milk.

4. Every time the child is given milk, ensure that the feeding bottle is properly washed and free from contamination to prevent the child from getting infected.
5. Efforts have to be made to ensure that right type of milk is used for feeding.

If the mother wishes to use dried milk powders for feeding the child then it is necessary to consult a pediatrician to get the recommendation for the baby food suitable for the child. There are several products available in the market to suit specic requirements of children of varying ages and physical condition and only an expert can decide on the product suitable for any particular child.

If the milk recommended by the doctor is not found suitable, then the mother should refer back to the doctor and get a fresh recommendation.

Weaning the Child

The baby should ideally be on the mother's milk for a period of two years. Every child has a right to be on breast-feeding for two years, which Allah has granted to it. Allah says in the The Holy Qur'an:

> *"Mothers should feed their milk to the children for two years."* (The Holy Qur'an, 2:233)

If the mother has to wean the child earlier than two years, she is permitted to do it but not earlier than twenty-one months of feeding.

Imam as-Sadiq says:

"The period of the mother feeding the child should be a minimum of twenty one months. If someone feeds the child for a lesser period, it will be causing a hardship to the child."[63]

In the two years of feeding by the mother, the child slowly gets used to consuming other types of food. In this period the mother can taper

---

[63] Wasail al-shiah, v15, p. 177

down the breast-feeding and substitute it with other nutritive foods.

After the period of breast-feeding is over the child is weaned. Now it will get ready to have other type of nutrition. Careful and informed mothers know the type of foods on which their children can be fed. These foods have to suit the nature of the child and should have good nutritive value.

Weaning the child from the breast is however not an easy task. For some days it will cry and crave for the breast-feeding. At this juncture the mother has to exercise a lot of patience and tact. The mothers sometimes try to apply some bitter material on their nipples or color the breasts black that the child develops an aversion for feeding on it. But care has to be taken not to scare the child. The child should not get a fear complex during weaning that it can have wrong effect on its health and psychology.

Daughter or Son

No sooner a woman becomes pregnant the speculation commences whether she will have a male or a female issue. She offers prayers for having a son. When her relatives come visiting her they say that the glow on her face indicates that she would get a son. Her adversaries say that her eyes indicate she is carrying a girl. The husband too wishes for a son. He occasionally expresses this desire to her. Prior to delivery the mind of every relative around in the maternity home wonders whether she will give birth to a boy or a girl.

When they come to know that the new arrival is a girl, sudden quiet descends on the gathering. But if it is a boy there will be instant shouts of joy. When the father hears of the birth of a boy, he becomes overjoyed. He will run to fetch sweets and fruits for the visitors. He issues instructions for taking good care of the child lest he caught cold. He starts pampering his wife and distributes gifts to the midwife and the attendants.

But, if the new arrival were a girl, his mien would drop. He would go and sit in a corner. He starts cursing his ill luck He thus makes his existence bitter. He neglects his convalescent wife and sometimes even talks of divorcing her. This is the state of affairs of our degenerate society. But there are always exceptions. There are parents who receive a daughter with open arms and affection as they do the son. But such families are in a minority.

Dear father and respected mother:

What difference it makes if you have a son or a daughter? Is a daughter less human than a son? Doesn't a daughter have the capacity to grow and progress? Can't she become a useful and valuable person? Is the daughter not your offspring? What special advantage the parents draw from a son that the daughter cannot provide them? If the daughter was not important in the eyes of Allah, then the progeny of the Holy Prophet would not have come through his daughter Fatima Zahra.

If you bring up the daughter properly she will not be any less than a son for you. If you see the pages of history you will nd references of women who were more capable than thousands of men.

Why this ignoble thinking in our society which has reduced the status of our women. There is need to carry on jihad against this evil. There is need to remove the thought of any difference between a son and a daughter. A daughter can be as useful and efcient a person as a son. You must receive the news of the birth of a healthy child, be it a son or a daughter, with equal happiness. You must thank God that it is a gift from Him that has come to you. It is a part of your existence that has come to the world.

The Prophet and his Holy Descendants always took this attitude towards the life.

Whenever the Imam Sajjad received the news of the birth of a child he never enquired if it was a son or a daughter. But he used to offer a prayer to Allah when he used to be informed that the new-born was hale and hearty.[64]

One day the Holy Prophet was busy talking to his companions when a person reached his presence and informed that Allah has given to him a daughter. He was joyful and offered his thanks to Allah. But when he saw the faces of his companions he found them crestfallen. He was upset with them and said, "What has happened to you? Allah has given to me a ower whose fragrance I smell. Allah has ensured sustenance for her too as He would for a son !"[65]

Allah has deplored the discrimination between the sons and daughters thus:

> *"When they get tidings of a daughter their faces turn dark with shame; anger pervades them and they hide their faces from others." (The Holy Qur'an, 16:58-59)*

---

[64] Wasail al-shiah, v15, p. 143

[65] Wasail al-shiah

Naming the Child

One of the prime responsibilities of the parents is the selection of a name for the new-born child. They should not treat this important thing as a triviality. Individuals and families are recognized with their names. If the name is affable the person will be well received by the people. Persons with unpleasant sounding names will not get good attention from others and sometimes even they might ridicule them. The persons who are given improper names will be victims of inferiority complex. Therefore Islam requires the parents to exercise care in selecting good names for their children.

The Holy Prophet has said:

"It is the responsibility of every father to choose a good name for his child."[66]

"The children have three rights over their fathers. The rst is that they are given good names. Secondly, they are provided good education; and lastly, they help them to select good spouses."[67]

Imam Musa al-Kadhim said:

---

[66] Wasail al-shiah, v2, p. 618

[67] Wasail al-shiah, v104, p. 92

'The rst good that a father does to his child is that he selects a worthy name for him."[68]

On the other hand the name of a person has a lot of social signicance too. It is his name, which gets recognition to a person that he belongs to a respectable family. If the parents have high regard for a well-known poet, they may name their child after him. If the parents are fond of high learning they may select the name of a reputed scholar.

The highly religious parents name their children after the prophets, the Imams and other religious personalities. If the parents desire their children to struggle in the cause of the faith, they name them after Muhammad, 'Ali, Hasan, Husayn, Abul Fadhl, Abbas, Hamza, Jaffar, Abu Dharr, Ammar, Saeed etc.

If the parents are enamored of any sport they like to name their children after renowned players of that sport. Similarly if the parents appreciate the art of any musician, they may prefer to name their child after that person.

When the nature of the parents is tyrannical, they take pride in naming the child after historical personalities like Alexander, Changes, Timor etc. It is noticed that while naming the child the parents generally associate themselves with certain groups and people of the past this will have a denite impact on the nature and thinking of the child when he grows up.

The Holy Prophet has said:

"Keep good names, because on the Day of Judgment you will be called by these names only. It will be proclaimed, 'so-and-so son of so-and-so Rise and get associated with your light, So-and-so, son of so-and-so Arise that there is no light for you that can guide you!'"[69]

One person said to Imam Ja'far as-Sadiq, "We name our children

---

[68] Wasail al-shiah, v15, p. 122

[69] Wasail al-shiah, v15, p. 123

after your name and the names of your revered ancestors. Is this benecial for us. "The Imam replies, "Yes By Allah's faith anything else than love for the pious and hate towards the profane!"

For the propagation of their beliefs people derive benet from every opportunity to project the names of the important personalities. They go to the extent of naming the towns, streets and other landmarks after important personalities. A responsible and devoted muslim too takes every opportunity to perpetuate the names of the great personalities of Islam and one of such acts is to name his children after them.

Yes Hasan, Husayn, Abul Fadhl, 'Ali Akbar, Hur, Qasim, Hamza, Ja'far, Abu Dharr, Ammar are amongst the names which enliven the spirit to remember the valiant acts of the great persons and encourage the coming generations to groom themselves on those models. When a person is named after the Holy Prophets like Ibrahim, Musa, Isa or Muhammad he is bound to have a feeling that he must try to be as righteous a person as he can. When a person is named after the friends and devotees of the Holy ahl al bait like Abu Dharr, Maithum and Ammar he will realise the signicance of the deeds of those great men. An intelligent Muslim will not give the names of tyrants and enemies of Islam to his children.

Imam Baqir says:

"Beware of the Satan When he hears that someone is called as Muhammad and 'Ali, he melts in such a way as the lead melts and when he hears that someone is named after one of our enemies he is overwhelmed with happiness."[70]

The Prophet of Islam said:

"Whoever gets four sons, and he has not named even one after me has been cruel on me."[71] Imam Muhammad Baqir said:

---

[70] Wasail al-shiah, v15, p. 127

[71] Ibid.

"The peerless names are the names of the Prophets."

The Holy Prophet attached so much importance to names that if he did not like the name of any companion or a place, he would immediately change the name. He changed the name of Abd al Shams to Abd al Wahab. He named Abd al Uzza (the slave of Uzza the idol) to Abd Allah. Abd al Haris (the tiger) to Abd ar Rahman and Abd al Ka'aba to Abd Allah.

Health and Hygiene

The dress of the child should be so designed that it suits the weather and the climate of the environment in which it is living. The dress should be such that the child should neither sweat during warm weather nor should it shiver during winter Soft and simple cottons are ideal for the child.

The clothes should not be tight tting which obstruct the movements of the child. Changing tight tting garments is inconvenient for the child and the mother nds it difcult putting them on or removing them. It is a practice among people that they pack the child in tight clothes that its limbs do not move.

Denitely, this is not a good practice and is harmful for the child. Doing this the freedom of the tiny baby is badly curbed. Such practice does hamper the normal growth of the child.

One author from the West writes:

"No sooner the child is delivered from the mother's womb, it wants to move its limbs and enjoy its freedom. This is when many mothers conne them to tight clothes. They rst stretch the limbs of the babies on the ground, wrap them with many cloths and tie a belt around them that they are unable to move. Thus the growth of the children, which has to be dynamic at this stage, slows down very much and they are stunted.

The countries where this uncivilized practice is not prevalent, the children have their normal growth and the people are generally robust, healthy and strong. To the contrary the areas where babies are tied up after birth there come about many deformities like lameness, dwarng etc. Can one imagine the impact of such upbringing on the mind and soul of the children?

The rst thought the child gets is of being a captive because it is not able to move freely. The condition of the child will be worse than that of a prisoner. Such children become irate and start crying and shouting. Imagine, if your limbs too are tied up, would you not cry and shout!"

The child too is a human being. It will have feelings and sensations. It also wishes to have freedom and

comfort. When its freedom is curbed by tying it up tightly it will naturally feel the pain. But it cannot defend itself and the only reaction it can show is that it starts crying. This creates pressure in the child's mind and in stages makes him excitable, peevish and short tempered.

The child's dress should always be kept clean. Whenever it wets the clothes, they must be immediately changed. The child's feet must be washed at intervals and the body given massage with olive oil so that it doesn't develop a dry skin. After a few wettings, the child should be given a bath. This way the child can be prevented from many ailments. Such a child will also appear clean, tidy and attractive to the eyes of the beholders.

The Prophet of Islam has said:

"Islam is the faith of purity. You must try to be pure and clean because only the clean can enter the Heaven."[72]

---

[72] Majma al-zawaid, v5, p.132

"Clean the children from oily dirt because the Satan smells them and they get scary dreams and the Angels get agitated."[73]

Circumcision of the male child is a mandatory Islamic custom. This is very important for the health and hygiene of the child. This operation will prevent the child against the possible infection of the male genital organ. The circumcision can be postponed till the child grows up, but it is better to perform it within the rst few days of the birth. Islam prescribes that the circumcision should be done on the seventh day of the birth of a male child.

Imam Ja'far as-Sadiq says:

"Do the circumcision of your child on the seventh day of his birth. This is best for him. It is also benecial for his proper growth and upbringing. Certainly, the earth abhors the urine of the person who has not been circumcised."[74]

The Holy Prophet says:

"The new born must be circumcised on the seventh day of its birth that he gets healthy growth and upbringing."[75]

Tonsuring the baby on the seventh day is prescribed in Islam. An equivalent of the weight of the tonsured hair in gold or silver has to be given in charity. On the same day as *aqiqa* a fat tailed ram (*dumba*) is butchered and the meat distributed to the poor and needy. They can also be invited to partake of it in a feast. The *aqiqa* is a good charity and will avert any evil in store for the child.

The new-born is very delicate. It needs all the care and attention of the parents. The foundation of health and happiness, or otherwise, will be laid in early childhood. The responsibility for this is on the shoulders of the parents. The parents, who are the cause of the child

---

[73] Bihar al-anwar, v104, p.95

[74] Wasail al-shiah, v15, p. 171

[75] Wasail al-shiah, v15, p. 175

coming to the world, bear theresponsibility to strive and bring it up as a robust, healthy human being. If the parents neglect this duty, they will be answerable for the consequences.

The child is always surrounded with the possibility of several illnesses. It can be prevented from them with good care. The ailments, which can affect the children, are infantile paralysis, boils on the body, measles, diphtheria, convulsions, kalazar etc. Preventive vaccinations against such ailments are given to the babies.

Generally paediatric hospitals have facilities of giving free preventive vaccinations to children against these diseases. The parents have no excuse to neglect their duty of getting timely preventive care for the children. If any disease aficts the child because of their carelessness, they will be answerable to Allah and their conscience too will ever curse them. It must be understood that it is the responsibility of the parents that they take good care of the health and well being of their children that they grow into t humans.

The Child's Sleep and Freedom of Movement

During the rst few weeks after the birth, the child sleeps most of the time. Approximately a new born sleeps for about 20 hours in a full day, but progressively the duration of waking hours increases. The need for total rest and sleep for a baby cannot be over stressed. Too much disturbance and noise makes the child restless and dgety. The child prefers a peaceful environment so that it can sleep comfortably.

Too much hugging, kissing and shifting from the arms of one person to another and bringing in too many visitors to see the baby will upset its tranquility. Noisy environment and blaring sounds of television and radio might affect the delicate nerves of the child. The sound sleep of the child should not be disturbed by careless behavior. It should not be moved around unnecessarily. If this practice is continued, over a period of time, the child will become short-tempered, excitable and peevish.

The newly born baby dislikes noisy surroundings and getting moved around. Care has to be exercised to see that its environment is kept noise free and the child is moved around only when it is absolutely necessary. The child prefers to be on the mother's lap or in its cradle, delicately swung, which makes it feel comfortable.

With the motion of the cradle the child feels that some caring person is around. If there is total quiet and there is no movement the child feels lonely. This is more so because the mother's womb is a cradle in which the child keeps moving and when it arrives in the world, it wants to move too. The mother's sweet lullabies too comfort the baby.

The child's rst year in the world is the period for the exercise of its body and limbs. The child likes movement for which it throws around the limbs. For this purpose the garments of the baby have to be loose tting and of soft fabric. Tying up a child in many layers of clothing will impede its free movement and will have ill effect on its nerves. Such children have no other alternative than crying which will be the precursor of rebellious and angry nature.

The Most Delicate Period of Life

The most delicate and crucial period of life is the childhood. The foundation for the future personality of the individual is established at this time. The slightest neglect might cause irreparable harm to the child's future personality and temperament. In fact, the rst three years of the child's life play a very crucial role in the metamorphosis of its personality and character.

Perhaps all, and denitely most, people don't realize this very important aspect of upbringing of a child. They generally say,

"Small children, and babies in particular, have no capacity to comprehend anything. They cannot speak and therefore are incapable of expressing their thoughts and feelings. They are so helpless that they even have no control over their bowels and hence have no capability to learn anything on their own".

With such an attitude the parents squander the period of early childhood of the baby. This is the most impressionable and delicate period of the child's life. During this apparently uncomplicated period the moral, cultural and religious instincts of the child take shape.

In this early three years' period the child picks up several hundred words and gets acquainted with their meanings. It will start distinguishing between good and bad, friendship and enmity, pretty and ugly, small and big; it will also get the faculty of identifying different colors, the taste of foods.

It develops the faculty of observation and speech. It starts showing rudiments of the thought process. It learns to crawl and walk. It will learn to laugh and to cry. During this three years' period there will be thousands of events that might affect the psyche of the child and have a bearing on its future temperament.

Despite all this, there will hardly be any person who can recall events of the rst three years of his life. All the events of the time will be under a cloud of oblivion and forgetfulness. But, all the same, those forgotten memories would already have had tremendous effects on the nature and personality of the individual. Several psychological ailments, fears, traumas, anger etc are the products of the events of the rst few years of the person's life.

One psychologist writes:

"If the child doesn't develop a strong personality in the early years of his life, then he will not have the capability to bear the onerous responsibilities which will confront him in the future. He will become the victim of several psychological defects. Therefore it is observed that the origin of nervous defects in a person can be traced to his childhood. ……..

Whenever a psychiatrist investigates the causes of any mental illness he draws an inference that the person had such conditions in his early childhood that are affecting the chances of his escape from his existing psychological problems."[76]

Dr Jalali writes:

"The foundation of the child's social behaviour is laid in the rst year

---

[76] Ruwan shinasi Khudak o baligh, p. 106

of its life. Its bent of mind becomes evident during this period only."[77]

Because of this, the responsible parents don't neglect this delicate and impressionable period in the child's life. They do not postpone the training of the child for the future. In fact the training and upbringing of the child commences with its birth.

Some intellectuals observe:

The child starts getting trained from its birth itself. The attention that the adults and other children around give him will be the rst step of his training. Similarly the scenes and anecdotes that the child experiences and the sounds that he hears will have impact on its subconscious and have a bearing on his learning experience. Several habits and experiences that are the building blocks of the person's character are connected with his childhood. Whatever attitude the parents adopt towards the child from its birth will have denite bearing on its upbringing and education.[78]

The time for commencement of moral training is the moment of the birth of the person. This is the time when the training commences without any possibility of failure. If the training is commenced later on, there will be likelihood of confronting negative attitudes in the child.[79]

'Ali told to his son, Imam Hasan

"The child's mind is like the virgin land. Whatever is put into it, will be accepted. Therefore, before your heart turned hard and engrossed otherwise, I took steps to make you polite."[80]

---

[77] Ruwan shinasi Khudak o baligh, p. 302

[78] Ilm al nafs al Tarbi, p. 19

[79] Dar tarbiat, p. 79.

[80] Wasail al-shia, p. 197

The Newborn and Moral Upbringing

When the child arrives in the world, it is very delicate. It has a mind but it does not think. It sees with its eyes but does not recognize the objects around it. It does not have the faculty to identify colors and faces. It will have no idea about distance. It hears sounds but is unable to comprehend them. Similar will be the condition of its other senses. But, despite all this, the child will have the faculty to use all these senses and going through the experiences it learns to use all of them.

Allah says in the Holy The Holy Qur'an:

> *"Allah has delivered you from your mother's wombs in such a condition that you knew nothing and endowed you with ears, eyes and hearts that, perhaps, you will become thankful." (The Holy Qur'an, 16:78)*

The main activities of a baby will be eating, sleeping, ailing its limbs crying and making water. For some weeks the baby is able to perform only these activities. Although the activities of a new born are few and very simple, it establishes a rapport with the other members of the family through these, it makes experiments, forms habits and acquires knowledge about himself and the things around him. These are the contacts and experiences that go to make the moral fabric of the person of the future.

'Ali has said: "As the days go by, the mysteries unravel."[81]

The child is a weak societal individual. Without others help it can neither be alive nor can nd sustenance. If others don't come to its rescue, and don't fulll its wants, it would perish. The persons in whose care is a baby, also are responsible for its complete upbringing including moral and religious training.

Thoughtful and caring parents, through their well-planned attitude, fulll the needs of the new arrival and provide the ideal environment for the growth of its body and soul. They infuse good morals and habits in the child. To the contrary, uninformed parents, through thoughtless actions create undesirable habits in the child.:

The new-born baby feels hungry and needs nutrition. It feels its need and looks to a Higher Being who can assuage its want. This is the reason the baby cries to attract the attention of the mother towards its need. If good care is taken to fulll the child's needs, on the basis of a well-planned schedule, then it will sleep comfortably and will wake up at the correct time when it has to be given the feed. The nerves of such properly attended babies are at ease. They get used to good and regular habits.

At this stage when the babies do not recognize anyone, will have their attention only on two things—their own frailty, helplessness and have their attention riveted on the Superior Power, which is Provider of all needs. They cry to get succour from that Hidden, Invisible Power that is the Creator of all things. The babies, on account of their frailty and inrmity, attach themselves to a Power that is Municent. If this

---

[81] Ghurar al-hukm, p. 47

feeling in the children is perpetuated, it will become the foundation of Belief, Faith and Spiritual contentment in their future.

The Prophet of Islam has said:

"Never beat the children if they cry. Fulll their needs. Because, for the rst four months of the life of a child, its cries are a witness to the Existence and Unity of Allah, Almighty."[82]

For the rst four months the newborn babies wouldn't have acquired the social entity. They would not recognize anyone, even their own mothers. This is the only period when the babies have their attention focused on one unseen Power. But those babies who are victims of the negligence of their mothers helplessly cry to attract attention for help. The nerves of such children will be disturbed and mostly they are restless. In stages the peevishness of these children become their second nature. There will be lack of self-condence in these children and they will be unruly and quarrelsome.

---

[82] Bihar al-anwar, v 104, p. 103

Religious Upbringing of the Newborn

It is a fact that the new born children are unable to comprehend the meaning of what is told to them but they denitely are able to identify the surroundings and the faces around them. They do hear the sounds and their senses and the minds take note of them. Therefore it is not correct to say that the newborn babies don't take any impression from what they see and what they hear in early childhood.

Although the new born are unable to understand the meaning of the talk going on around them, the sounds of the words are registered on their minds and in stages they start to understand the meanings and they become a part of their vocabulary. Even amongst adults it is noted that the words which impress the mind most are retained in the memory. The adults recognize well-known persons easier than casual or occasional acquaintances.

Similarly the new born baby too, living in a spiritual environment, hearing the recitation of the Holy Book, the word of Allah coming to their ears and having seen the parents offering prayers in their presence will develop into religiously upright persons. On the other hand the new born babies who are surrounded by irreligious persons, hear the sounds of uncivil and abusive language, are exposed to amoral music and songs, will no doubt grow up to be persons similar to those in whose company they are growing up.

Intelligent and thoughtful parents will not waste any opportunity of training their children. They go to the extent that they take care to see that the children get to hear only good sounds and see good things.

The prophet of Islam too has given his view on this important aspect of training of the children. He has said:

"No sooner the child is born, recite the *adhan* (the Call for Prayer) in the right ear and the *iqamah* (the Call to rise for offering the Prayer) in the left."

'Ali narrates from the Holy Prophet:

"When a child is born in any family, the *adhan* should be recited in the child's right ear and the *iqamah* in the left ear that the child is protected from the evil of the Satan. He (The Prophet) gave the same instruction at the birth of Imam Hasan and Imam Husayn. In addition he asked for recitation of ayat al Kursi, the nal verses of Hashr, al Ikhlas, al Nas, and al Falaq to reach the child's ears."[83]

In some traditions it is narrated:

"The Holy Prophet himself recited the *adhan* and the *iqamah* in the ears of Imam Hasan and Imam Husayn at their birth."

Yes. The Holy Prophet was aware that a child is not able to comprehend the meanings of *adhan* and *iqamah* recited into its ears, but the impact of the words which will be there on the mind of the new-born was not over looked. The Prophet was stressing on the point that these pious words would have salutary effect on the mind and spirit of the new arrival.

Perhaps, the Holy Prophet was intending to instruct the parents about the proper upbringing of their children, that they commence

---

[83] Mustadrak al-wasail,v2, p. 619

their task right from the birth of the child. When a thoughtful parent recites the *adhan* in his child's ear, then he is proclaiming that he is attaching his child to the group of worshippers of Allah.

The effects the child takes in its early days are not related to the sense of hearing only. But, it can be said that whatever exposure the child's other senses get will impact its mind and memory. For example, if a child witnesses any amoral act, although it may not understand the purport of the act, it will denitely have effect on its psyche.

This is the reason the Holy Prophet has said:

"If the child in the cradle is seeing, the man should refrain from copulating with his wife."[84]

---

[84] Mustadrak al-wasail, v 2, p. 546

The Sense of Belonging

The newly born baby will be a delicate identity who cannot live on without support from others. When he was in the mother's womb, he had a warm and cozy corner for himself, where the nutrition and warmth was provided by the mother. He had no concern for any needs. Now that he has arrived into the world, he has started to feel dependent. The rst need the baby feels is, perhaps, the need for warmth because the environment it has come into is cooler. Then he feels the need for satisfying its hunger.

For the rst time it knows that for warmth and food he has to depend on others. At this stage he doesn't know any one who can help. By nature he is aware of his needs and focuses his attention on an unseen Power to satisfy these needs. From the very beginning of his life the child is possessed with this sense of belonging, and this sense will be there with him throughout life.

When the child feels hungry or thirsty, it cries. It will cling to the bosom of the mother and feels soothed with the lullabies sung by her. If the child gets the feeling of any danger around him, he clings to the apron strings of the mother.

This sense of belonging which later on manifests itself in the habit of following the lead (taqlid) of others. The child models his morals and behavior on the morals and attitudes of the persons in his immediate surroundings. This sense of belonging which later on helps the child to make friends and play with his mates. The fraternity and affection towards the spouse and his own children are a natural continuation of the sense of belonging. This development in the child is the precursor of the gregarious nature of human beings.

Therefore the sense of belonging that a child has is no triviality and is the most important aspect of the structure of the human society. The child develops the faculty of hope and contentment. He will develop the feeling of camaraderie towards others, he thinks good of others and expects their co-operation.

When his opinion about the society is good, then he would extend his hand in support to it and make the necessary sacrices towards this end. The people in the society will consider him as their well-wisher.

Contrary to this, if the sense of belonging is suppressed, and is not utilized rightly, then the child might deviate from the straight path that God has assigned for him. The view of the psychologists is that at many stages the child, on account of the happenings in its environment, might get the rudiments of feeling of fear, restlessness, lack of condence, shame, loneliness, sadness and even suicidal tendencies.

If you want to satisfy the sense of belonging of the child properly, then always try to be its supporter. When it is hungry, feed it. Provide means of comfort to it. If the child has any discomfort or pain, try to ameliorate it. Keep his program of sleep and feed in control in such a way that it has no inconvenience.

Avoid beating the child. The child doesn't know anything other than its immediate needs. It only trusts an Unknown Power and it cries seeking the help of that Power. Don't take out your ire on the child by beating it.

The Holy Prophet says:

"Do not beat the babies when they cry, because when a child under the age of four months cries, it is bearing witness to the Unity of Allah."[85]

Be a supporter of the child under all circumstances, even if you are unable to perform a task for him, try to treat him with love and care. If the child is uncomfortable, try to remove the cause of the discomfort. Never reprimand the child and threaten him that you would leave him alone and go away. Doing such acts might affect the child's psychology.

The child expects to be the cynosure of the eyes of the parents. If they don't show affection to the child, it will be very upset. The child always tries to get the love and affection of the parents. Some parents make a wrong use of this tendency and tell him that if he did not obey them, they would not love him. They should avoid using this pretence.

These subterfuges might ultimately affect the psyche of the child in stages. If the child cries, it can also be to attract the attention of the parents. The parents should handle the child with patience and thoughtfulness. If the child is admonished or beaten when it cries, it might quieten for the moment, but this will be the quietness of disappointment which might have dangerous impact on its mind.

The child is always happy with the parents around and is uncomfortable when they are away. The parents should never talk about their death in the hearing of the child that will be very upsetting and disturbing for him. A sick parent should not mention possibility of his death in the presence of the child. If a parent has to travel away from the child for a considerably long period, prepare the child for the event. While away, maintain contact regularly.

When a child refuses to take medicine, don't frighten it by saying that if it did not comply, it would die. Take a positive attitude and try to

---

[85] Bihar al-anwar, v104, p.104

console and convince him to take the medicine to get well. If the child is suffering from a serious ailment, maintain calm and composure in its presence. The parents should always try to be good friends and well wishers of the child throughout their lives.

It should be borne in minds that the expression of love and affection for the child should be moderate. Pampering a child might be harmful for it in a long run. Wherever a child is unable to perform a task, the parents should assist it. But when the child is capable of doing a thing by itself, the parents should leave it alone to accomplish it. Sometimes, a child might try to get attention of others by crying despite having the capability of performing its own task. In such an event, it should be ignored.

Russell writes:

"If the child cries for no reason, then it should be left to its own scruples and allowed to cry as much as it could. If any other attitude is adopted in such circumstances, the child might become dictatorial and misbehave more often. Whenever a child cries for a genuine need, the attention given should not go to the extent of pampering it."[86]

---

[86] Dar tarbiat, p. 79

When the Child Starts to See the World Around Him

The child is a man in miniature and its nature too will be social. It needs the help and support of others to live. It will have its attention focused on others; it derives benet from them and provides benets to them in return. But for a few months the newborn does not recognize others and is not capable of giving them any attention.

By the time it is four months old the rudiments of social nature start showing in his acts. From this time it gives attention to the surroundings and starts observing the action of its mother. It starts reacting to the acts of the mother. If the mother smiles, it smiles back. If the mother moves her eyebrows, it does the same in return. It looks at the toys with interest and smiles. It starts gauging others feelings of happiness and anger. It is taken aback at the slightest expression of anger.

When the child is confronted with happy and bright faces it jumps towards them. It wants to sit up and look at the world around it.

At this stage the parents should take care with realization that the child has developed a sense of the surroundings and is a full-edged member of the family. The child is able to give attention to the others in the family and is, to an extent, able to understand their feelings. In the four months of its life the child has gone through experiences and experiments and has acquired memory for things around him.

This is the dawn of the future social being in him. If the parents are thoughtful in trying to nurture this instinct in the child, he can be helped to develop into a useful member of the society. Otherwise, the child starts becoming oblivious of the outside world and becomes restricted to the valley of its own inner world. He can turn into an introvert and becomes a recluse. He will become a victim of inferiority complex.

The parents therefore carry an onerous responsibility. They should be aware that the child has feelings and takes effect of their behavior. They must keep their attention focused on him. They should come to the presence of the child with a smiling and pleasant face. They should talk with the child affectionately. They should provide to the child educational toys so that it gets acquainted with the outside world with ease and comfort.

If the felt needs and desires of the child are fullled, it will feel comfortable. It starts feeling that others wish him well and are his benefactors. When he receives good treatment, the child gets ready to be a good member of the society. Good and thoughtful parents don't beat the children nor do they treat them harshly. They are aware that such attitude will have adverse effect on the mind of the child and render him a defeatist and timid person.

The Prophet of Islam has said:

"Respect your children and give them a good upbringing that Allah blesses you."[87]

---

[87] Makarim al-akhlaq, p. 255

Affection

Man is ever thirsty for love and affection. Love gives life. to hearts. One, who loves oneself wishes that others too should have similar feelings for him, feels happy in his heart. When a person feels that none in this world loves him: feels forlorn and hapless. He will therefore be always sad and melancholy. The child too is a man in miniature and, in fact, needs more love and affection than the adults. As the child needs nutrition, so does he need love and affection?

The child does not care if he is living in a palace or a shack. But he knows it pretty well whether he is getting the love and affection of his companions or not. From the feeling of love and care the child proceeds on the path of growth and well being. The fountainhead of good character is love and affection. Under the reection of love the feelings and thoughts of a child can be nurtured properly to make him a good human being.

The child who receives profuse love will have a happy spirit and heart. He will not be a victim of disappointment. He will turn into a person who is condent, good-natured and self-respecting. He will not become a victim of psychological problems. The children who have received the love and affection of the elders are better prepared to face the harsh realities and problems of the adult life.

A girl who has received the love and affection of her parents, and her household, is endowed with the aura of affection, will not succumb to the overtures of a boy in her youth that might affect her future life. A boy who had his upbringing in the atmosphere of true love and affection will not become victim of evils like drugs and drinking.

From the psychological point of view too it is proven that the children who have received profound love and affection of their parents during their growing years are more intelligent and healthy than those who grow in dormitories away from their parents. It is another thing that children from boarding schools may have better nutrition and health care.

But those who have their upbringing in a mechanical atmosphere devoid of feelings of love and affection, and have not experienced close comfort of the company of the Parents, may not have the natural feelings of affection towards others.

A child who has not fully shared the love and affection of his parents will be a victim of the feeling of deprivation and inferiority. Mostly the cause of anger, shamelessness, short temper, depression etc is the lack of the parents love and affection during the childhood of the person.

The persons who turn to evils like theft and murder in most cases were devoid of parental love and affection in their early lives. They behave like the rebels of the society. They may even have suicidal tendencies. The newspapers and magazines are replete with stories of such unfortunate persons.

Dr Hasan Ahdi, chief of the Division of Psychiatry, of The National Society for Care of Children (*Anjuman Melli Himayat Bachhagan*), has conducted an experiment on ve hundred convicts and concluded that the persons committed the rst crime at the ages between 12 and 13.

The main cause of the delinquency has been lack of love and affection from their families.

He says:

"The rudiments of most of the psychological problems can be traced to the childhood. Even the most balanced child has the problem of allaying his emotions."[88]

A young person writes:

"I opened my eyes in a poor family in a small village. The upkeep of my two sisters and me was beyond the means of my parents. My grand mother took me to her home. Her circumstances were better. She loved me very much. She used to buy good dresses and other things for me.

But these comforts were no substitute for the love and affection of my mother and father that I wanted. I used to feel as if I had lost something. Many a time I used to cry inconsolably hiding from others view. I was a student of the Third Standard then. Once my father came to meet me. He asked me to come home. I was overjoyed at the prospect and immediately got ready to go.

I felt as if my troubles of years have come to an end in a moment. I advise all fathers and mothers not to deprive their children of their presence, love and affection by sending them away howsoever straitened the circumstances. They must realize that living away from the parents and being deprived of their personal love and affection will be very hard on the children. This void cannot be lled by any amount of comforts."

He writes in another letter:

"I was deprived of the love and affection of my parents. That is the reason I am now a heart broken jealous person. I am a cowardly and angry person. In childhood I used to run away from my school. With

---

[88] Daily Kihan, Issue 42

difculty I could reach till the Sixth Standard at the school and then dropped out."

The Holy Faith of Islam, which provides great care to the process of upbringing of children, makes particular stress to love and affection for the children. The The Holy Qur'an and Hadith has volumes on the subject. Here, a few examples are sited:

Imam Ja'far as-Sadiq has said:

"Because of the profound love that the parents have for their children, Allah will include them in His Blessings. (Grace)."[89]

Allah has said to the Prophet Moses (in a hadith al-qudsia): "Loving children is the best of acts because the purpose of their creation is for worship of Allah and witnessing the Unity of Allah. If the children die in their childhood, they would enter the Heaven. (Mustadrak al-wasail,v2, p. 615)

The Prophet of Islam said:

"Love children and be kind to them."[90]

"Kiss your children profusely, because every time you kiss the child, Allah will advance your position in the Heaven by one stage."[91]

One person told to the Prophet:

"I have not kissed any child till today."

When that person left the company of the Prophet, he told to his companions, "In my view the person is destined for the Hell."[92]

"A person who is not kind to children and not respectful to elders is not from amongst us."[93]

'Ali, while making his will and last testament said:

---

[89] Wasail al-shia, v15, p. 98

[90] Bihar al-anwar, v104, p. 92

[91] Bihar al-anwar, v104, p. 92

[92] Bihar al-anwar, v104, p. 99

[93] Bihar al-anwar, v75, p. 147

"Be kind to children and respectful to your elders."[94]

---

[94] Bihar al-anwar, v75, p. 146

The Expression of Love and Affection

Love for one's own children is a natural instinct. Perhaps there will be few parents who don't love their children from the depths of their hearts. But only loving the child from the heart is not sufcient for the betterment of the child. The child needs love that is reected in the actions of the parents.

The child wants to be kissed, hugged and to be looked at with caring smiles. When the parents sing the lullabies, the child savors their sweetness. The child desires that the parents play with and gambol with him. The child treats this as a sign of love. It considers the anger and conicts as signs of thoughtlessness. Whenever the parents look at the child at different times, it visualizes at that moment if there is a look of love on their faces or not.

There are also parents who shower their love on the child till it is a baby. But as it grows up, they gradually reduce the expression of love and when the child reaches adolescence and adulthood they totally forsake him and even say that any more expressions of love might spoil him. But this is not the right attitude.

The child expects the love of his parents throughout his life. He feels joy over the expression of love by the parents and if he nds them ignoring him, he has a feeling of hurt. Particularly the adolescence is a very critical period in the life of a person when support and guidance of the parents is required the most. It is this neglect of the adolescent-adults by their parents that there are many cases of suicide in this age group. There are also cases of such persons eeing to some unspecied place. It won't be out of place here to quote some entries from the diary of Nazneen, a teenager:

"When I think of my mom and dad I cannot but laugh. Although they deserve more to be sadly pitied than laughed at Mom is busy in her own world, occupied with her daily chores. She wants to sit gossiping for hours at end with Aunt Vizri Jaan and Lady Hamida. If some of us sisters and brothers arrive in the midst of these conversations for some errand, she abhors the interruption. She doesn't realize that while gossiping about the idiosyncrasy of others' footwear and attire she makes me feel like a bird who is uttering around to pour its heart's feeling to someone.

Mom and Dad are either busy arguing with one another or sitting with friends for society gossip. Or otherwise, they are away from home. I am also busy at the school from morning to evening on all working days. It is since many days that I have set eyes on Dad. My teacher of Literature is a psychologist.

Today he talked on the effect that a father can have on the psyche of his daughter. His talk went straight to my heart. He was right in saying that I am a grown up in the eyes of everyone. But I feel the need of the guidance of my dad more than at any other time in my life. There is need for the moral strength of someone wise and kind. But he, my Dad, seems to have no time for this."[95]

The best place for the training of a child, particularly in the early stages of life, is the home. In this period the child receives total

---

[95] Daily Itallaat, Issue 14112, Khurdad Month 1358

attention, kindness and love of the parents. The parents are advised that as far as possible they don't entrust their small children to the care of crèches.

Perhaps, these crèches may be better equipped for hygiene and nutrition but they provide a cold and strange environment to the child. The place will be like a goal for the child who wants the company of the parents more than anything else. Only good environs and nutrition cannot ll the void created by the absence of the love and care of the parents.

The Prophet of Islam has observed:

"If you like someone, express your feelings to him. This expression of love brings you closer to each other."[96]

The Prophet used to play with his children and grand children every morning expressing his love and affection for them.[97]

---

[96] Mustadrak al-wasail,v 2, p. 67

[97] Mustadrak al-wasail,v 104, p. 99

Love – Not an Instrument of Convenience

Because the child needs the love and affection of the parents, some parents make use of this urge of the children for their own ends. They ask the child to do a certain thing that the mom would love him and ask him not to do certain things or otherwise mom would not love him. No doubt, a certain degree of control can be exercised on the child's action in this manner. But continuing with this strategy for long can be detrimental.

The child will get into the habit of doing things only to please the parents and not for any benet for him and the society at large. He starts deciding the reason for doing any work with the sole purpose of pleasing someone. He doesn't get the realization that his actions have to be tuned to the welfare of the society and the humanity in general.

There are lots of parents who value personal benet more than the good of the society. Their children become unkies, atterers, hypocrites and impostors because their purpose in life becomes pleasing others at any cost. Therefore, a clever and thoughtful mentor wouldn't use the love and affection of the child for selsh ends.

Love Should Not Become A Hindrance to Good Upbringing

There are parents who will love their children to such an extent that they don't realize what is good and what is bad for their upbringing. When they notice any fault in the child, or when someone else points out the fault, they overlook it not to displease the child. You must have seen such children who hurt other children, trouble other persons, break windowpanes in the neighborhood and use abusive language with others. The parents of such children not only ignore to correct them, but they also keep a phlegmatic smile on their faces as if the child has done nothing wrong.

Thus they abet the undesirable acts of the children. They do a great disservice to their own children. This neglect of proper upbringing is not pardonable in the eyes of Allah. Love for the children doesn't mean that the parents close their eyes to the norms of good upbringing.

Good parents are those who make a clever mix of love and good upbringing. They love the children and keep a realistic eye on the behavior of the child. They cleverly try to correct the faults of the child. They make the child realize that he is not free to do wrong acts. He is made aware of the fact that if the parents love him for the good things he does; he may be punished for anything wrong committed by him.

The parents have to realize that the child will grow into an adult and will have to interact with others in the society. If, because of their extreme love for the child, they have neglected their duty of training him in the norms of good behavior, he will not be welcome in the society and others will avoid him or even hate and abhor him. It must be borne in minds that other people will not be like the parents who close their eyes to every fault of the child and continue loving him. In the society a person is accepted for his good behavior only.

Imam Muhammad Baqir says:

"The worst father is that who loves his child beyond limits."[98] 'Ali, The Commander of the Faithful, says:

"One who has been taught good manners, his faults have been reduced."[99] Imam Muhammad al Baqir said:

"My revered father saw a person going with his son. The impolite son was reclining on the arm of his father. My father, Imam Zain al Abidin, was so upset with the impertinent child that for the rest of his life he didn't talk to him."

---

[98] Yaqubi, Tarikh, v2, p. 320

[99] Ghirar al-hukm, v2, p.645

The Spoilt Child

This is a reality that every child wants love and affection; but excess of love borders on pampering. Love is like food and in optimum measure it is very benecial but excess of it will be harmful in many ways.

Excessive pampering and mollycoddling will adversely affect the upbringing of the child. The child is not a plaything for the parents and nor should it be treated as a source of recreation by them. The child , in fact, is a precursor of the man of the future. It has to be brought up carefully and methodically. The responsibility for the upbringing, training and education of the child rests with the parents.

The child grows into an adult and has to be a part of the society. It will have to face the ups and downs of life, successes, failures, rise, fall, happiness and sorrow as it goes along in its life span. A good mentor will have all these factors in mind and prepare the novice to capably confront all the tests and hurdles which might confront him. The parents should be aware of the fact that love and affection is essential for good breeding of the child but excess of these can also come in the way of the desired results. The children who get excess of love and affection are likely to be spoilt with very harmful consequences.

When a child realizes that the parents love it very much, always allow him to have his own way, then naturally his demands will increase by leaps and bounds. He gets into the habit of ordering and expecting tacit compliance from the parents who are not willing to displease him. In such children the tendency of despotism keeps increasing with passage of time. When such persons enter the ranks of the society they expect the same compliance from their fellow citizens, as they did with the parents and other members of the family. But people don't like self-seeking persons nor do they take cognizance of their wishes.

This attitude of the people dampens the spirit of the selsh persons and they become the victims of the feeling of defeat and ennui. They develop a strong feeling of inferiority complex and tend to become recluses. In acute cases they think of committing suicide to escape from the psychological pressures that go beyond their ken.

The marital lives of such persons too are generally on the rocks. Such persons expect too much love from their spouses and expect them to comply with all their wishes, howsoever unreasonable they might be. But in practical lives, there is always the need of give-and-take and seldom there are any spouses who submit to one way trafc in their lives.

There are innumerable wives who take cudgels against unreasonable attitudes adopted by their husbands. The result is domestic unrest. Similarly a pampered daughter, when married, expects greater love from her husband than he has for his parents. She expects him to meet all her demands without giving a thought to their reasonableness.

Generally men do not like complying with all the wishes of such nagging wives. The result, naturally, is constant bickering in the family. Such men and women are also seen who continue the childish habit of quarrelling in their advanced ages. Such persons are so immature that they continue to behave like small children in their adult days.

The children getting their upbringing with over-indulgent, pampering parents are generally of delicate constitution and frail physique. They generally look for the support of others and are not independent. Whenever they face any hardship, they look for avenues of escape. They lack courage of taking up big and difcult tasks. If faced with difculties, they look for succour from others than depending on their own selves and on Allah.

The persons who have received over-indulgent upbringing are generally egotistic and self-centered. Having received supercial praises in their early days, they assume false airs of importance during their adult life. They are not able to discern their own failings and, to the contrary, think that these very lacunae are their merits. They work under a false sense of pride, which in itself is a grave psychological ailment.

'Ali has said:

"Self-conceit (egotism) is the worst thing."[100]

"A person who is an egoist and is living within himself, will become aware of his own aws and failings."[101]

Such a person expects others to heap on him their false praises. He will therefore have sycophants and atterers around him. But the forthright and true persons will not have any place in his company. The egoists, instead of winning devotion of others, generally invite their ire.

Imam 'Ali has said:

"Whoever is an egoist and self-centered will be confronted with lot of difculties."[102]

The children who receive excessive love and care and their parents

---

[100] Ghirar al-hukm, p. 446

[101] Ghirar al-hukm, p.685

[102] Ghirar al-hukm, p.659

are overindulgent towards them, they will in stages dominate the parents. When they grow into adults, they persist with the dominating trait and their expectations surpass the means of the parents.

If the parents express their inability to meet their demands, they have recourse to lots of hullabaloo to get their way. Because such children are aware of the overindulgence of the parents, they always have recourse to lies to get what they wish to have.

Parents at times come to such a pass that out of their love they overlook the need for good upbringing and indulge the child's whims and fancies. They close their eyes to the failings of the child and neglect the need for reforming him. To humor the child, the parents sometimes overlook the norms xed by the religion (shariah)

Imam Muhammad Baqir says:

"The worst father is one who exceeds unreasonably in the love for his child."[103]

The child should always live in optimism and fear (of God). He should have the feeling that truly he is the beloved of the parents and they would come to his rescue in times of need. He should also be made aware of the fact that for any fault of his the parents would hold him accountable.

Dr. Jalali writes:

"If a child lives in an environment where he is pampered, always others take sides with him, close their eyes to his wrong deeds and he is not groomed for the harsh realities of the future; he will then be subject to many hardships as a member of the society. From his very birth the child has to be trained that he has to exist with others in the society and his wishes have to be in harmony with the wishes of others in the society."[104]

---

[103] Ghirar al-hukm, p.659

[104] Ruwan shinashi kudak, p. 354

Dr Jalali also writes:

"Love for the child is essential. But the feeling in a child that the parents spend all their time humoring him is not right."[105]

If the child cries unnecessarily and expresses anger to win the attention of the parents to fulll his unfair demands, then the parents should rmly and tactfully deny compliance. They should leave him alone for a while for him to realize that he cannot always get his way. If the parents exercise some patience in such situations, the child will become quiet after some protestation.

If a child falls on the ground, it is not necessary to pick him up or console him. Let the child rise himself when he falls down. Train him to take care that he does not fall again. When a child hits his head against a wall by accident, it is not necessary to kiss him or over-indulge him. Instead, he should be trained to take care of himself against such happenings again.

When a child is indisposed, medical treatment should be arranged for him. Proper attention should be given to the child's illness, but daily chores should be attended to as usual. The parents should have their rest, sleep and food as normally as possible by not spending all their time near the bed cuddling the sick child. This behavior over indulgence doesn't help in any way, but it can aggravate the child's habit of craving for the attention of the parents.

A lady writes:

"After the rst two daughters my parents had their rst son. I cannot forget the celebratory mood of my mother at that time. My parents pampered my sibling so much that at the age of two years he used to beat us sisters. He used to bite us and we had no courage to defend ourselves. Whatever he desired was made available to him without any fuss. He used to be naughty with other children.

---

[105] Ruwan shinashi kudak, p. 461

For going to school he was shown lot of indulgence. But he used to avoid doing any schoolwork. He never paid the slightest heed to his teachers. He never progressed and ultimately dropped out of school. Now that he is a grown up adult, he is an uneducated and lonely person. He takes no interest in any work and has become very excitable. He has no love for his sisters.

Our dear brother has become a victim of the faulty upbringing and excessive indulgence of our parents!"

Sucking of Thumbs

It is the common habit of small children that they suck their thumbs. Generally at three months age the babies commence thumb sucking and keep doing it for some time. The natural cause of this habit can be the breast-feeding of the baby. When it is hungry it either suckles the breast of the mother or the rubber-soothers.

The child feels that sucking gives it comfort and over a time learns that it can suck its thumb when the mother's breast is not available to it. This is a part of the learning process of the child. It detects the usefulness of sucking its thumb and gets used to the habit.

This habit comes handy to the child when it is hungry and the feed is not available to it; also it can allude to thumb sucking if it has any feeling of discomfort. Many parents think that thumb sucking is not a good habit and devise ways of stopping the child from doing it. Here it must be mentioned that orthodontists consider thumb sucking adversely affects the natural conguration of teeth and the mouth, many dentists and doctors have felt that thumb sucking in children is not so harmful.

One expert says:

"Many psychologists and pediatricians opine that thumb sucking habit in children is not harmful in any way and in most instances it doesn't become the cause of any defect in the mouths. They also observe that this habit tapers off automatically once the child has set its milk teeth."[106]

But, nevertheless it is possible that this habit might cause some health problems because generally the child's ngers are exposed to the atmosphere and might carry some infectious material into the mouth. Most parents therefore don't want their child to get into the habit of thumb sucking.

Apparently this habit of thumb sucking is not a serious problem and if a child gets used to it, the habit will leave him as he grows up. But if the parents want, they can take steps to see that the child does not get into the habit at the initial stages. Preventing a child from the habit of thumb sucking is far easier than stopping it after it has got habituated.

When the parents initially notice the tendency of thumb sucking in the child, they should try to nd the reason, give it more milk if its hunger is not satiated, and if it gets hungry between the feeding schedule give it some fruit juice or biscuit. But if the reason for thumb sucking is some discomfort, it must be properly investigated and remedy found. If the child gets into the habit of thumb sucking despite all the preventive steps, then it will be difcult to check the habit.

Another method of checking this habit in children is to provide them with good and soft toys with a view to divert their mind from thumb sucking. If the child is provided company of some other child to play with, it might not suck the thumb during the time they are at play. The other alternative tool for avoiding thumb sucking is to give the child a rubber-soother to suck. But here too there will be a chance

---

[106] Ruwan shinashi kudak, p. 172

of the child getting habituated to the tool for a period of time.

However, the parents have to practice patience and restraint in checking this habit in children and they should not have recourse to punishing the child to the detriment of its psyche. The parents should bear in mind that however strong the habit of thumb sucking in a child, it will leave him by about four or ve years of age.

Fear

Fear is a universal phenomenon. Every living creature has the instinct of fear to a lesser or greater extent. In abstract terms fear is essential for the safety of human beings. A person who doesn't have the instinct of fear is not a psychologically normal person. This is the fear which makes man run away from dangerous calamities and save himself from death. Therefore, fear is a blessing that God has infused in the nature of human beings. But this blessing is useful only when man utilises it judiciously. Otherwise it will bring about harmful results. Fear manifests itself in two main forms:

First: Imaginary, misplaced and inane fears.

Second: Meaningful, reasonable and legitimate fears.

Inane Fears

The rst category of inane fear can be the fear of devils, evil spirits; fear of the darkness, fear of harmless animals like cats, rats, frogs, camels, horses. Fear of thieves and burglars, fear of cadavers, the cofns; fear of the doctor and the shots he injects, fear of the lightning and fear of sleeping alone; fear of the examinations; fear of disease and death.

There are a lot of such baseless fears that can become the bane of a person if he is not able to overcome them.

He is always obsessed with the fears and wakes up sometimes from sleep shouting and yelling as a result of seeing disturbing and horrendous dreams. Unnecessary fear and tension is a psychic illness that can have very harmful effects on the child's future life. A timid person will lack courage and while taking any major decisions he will be subject to great pressure. He will avoid meeting people and will always be worried and crestfallen. He will run away from congregations and will prefer a lonely existence. Several psychic illnesses spring from such inane fears in a person.

'Ali, The Commander of the Faithful, says:

"Fear is calamitous."[107]

Therefore a good mentor will makes efforts to see that the child remains free of unfounded fears. We have some suggestions here for the consideration of the mentors:

1. Preventing fears is far better than curing them. Try to ensure that the child is not exposed to situations of unfounded fears that it turns timid. Psychologists observe that the sound of a running locomotive, lightning, thunders, sound of alarms and noises near the head of a baby can be the initial causes of fear in a child. As far as possible protect the child from such exposures.
2. Fear is infectious. The child by nature is not timid. But if the parents and others in his environment are timid, then the child gets into this habit. If you wish that your child had no fears, then seek a cure for your own fears. Don't express fear over unfounded causes of fear.
3. Watching lms on the subject of crime and punishment, watching

---

[107] Gharar al hukm, p. 8

and listening to horror stories on the television and radio, reading and hearing mystery stories and even reading accounts of fearsome events in the papers and journals can be harmful for the children. As far as possible keep the impressionable children away from such things. Never talk about the Jinns and fairies to the children. If they have heard from some quarters about these, convince them that the existence of the Jinns is conrmed by the The Holy Qur'an but they also lead lives like the human beings and don't do us any harm.

4. Abstain from intimidating the child for his training. Don't frighten him with mention of the devil and evil spirits. These methods might be effective momentarily but they can render the child timid. As a punishment for misdemeanor the child should never be conned to a lonely dark corner. Some thoughtless mothers produce the sound of a cat or a dog from behind a wall to quieten their crying children. They don't know the harm such things might cause to the impressionable mind of the little child. A person writes in his diary:

"Our grandma was in the habit of going to another room in the house and shouting in a changed tone,' I am the devil have come to your house to eat you !"We used to fall quiet with fear and in the belief that it was really the devil. Over a period of time such acts rendered me a timid person. This is the reason that I cannot stir alone out of my house. I am now a timid and nervous adult"

One woman writes:

"I was around ve years then. I was playing one day in the courtyard with my cousin. Suddenly we noticed a horrible apparition. It had a big head, shining eyes, big long teeth, long and lose black dress and big black shoes in its feet. It was in the middle of the courtyard. Making weird sounds it wanted to gobble us. We yelled and ran into the dark attic. I clawed the wall with such intensity that my fingers were bruised. I fell unconscious with fear.

I had to be rushed to the doctor to revive me. For a long time I used to hide myself in corners with fear and the slightest commotion would upset my nerves. Even now I have shattered nerves and am unable to concentrate on any activity. Later on I learnt that the apparition was a practical joke of another of my cousins. She put a painted earthen pot over her head to frighten us out of our wits. She has become the cause of my nervous condition."

1. If your child is timid because of your carelessness or other causes, then don't neglect his condition any further. Try to rectify the situation as soon as possible. If the child realizes that his fears are unfounded, he will become normal by himself. But shouting at the child and ridiculing him and putting him to shame in front of others is no solution for the problem.

Such acts on the one hand do not remove the child's fears and on the other hand make him morose and despondent. He doesn't want to remain timid. Your carelessness and other causes have made him timid. Try to find the causes of his fears with patience and thoughtfulness. Then search for remedies.

If the child is afraid of imaginary devils and evil spirits, convince him that there are no such things. Tell him that the Jinns have nothing to do with the humans. If the child fears the harmless animals, demonstrate to him practically that the animals are harmless. If the child is scared of darkness, acquaint him with places with reduced lighting. When you are yourself with the child, momentarily put off the light. Then progressively increase the period of darkness. When you are in the same room with the child at some distance, repeat the experiment of putting off and switching on the lights. Repeat these trials with patience till the fear of darkness is removed from the mind of the child.

Remember No harsh methods should be employed to correct the fear complex of the child. Forcing a child to face the things he fears will have negative results. If the child is afraid of going to the doctor and taking vaccinations then convince him with love and affection about the need for the treatment. Sometimes the situation demands that the child has to be admitted to a pediatric hospital. It will be a difcult time that the child does not like to be away from the parents. If the child is forced to admit in the hospital against his wish, it can be very difcult on him Sometimes it is useful to acquaint the child with the environment of a hospital.

When the parents go visiting a patient in a hospital, they should take the child there for a short visit that he gets acquainted with the environment. Meeting the kind doctors and nurses in the hospital will remove the fear from the child's mind and in the event of his needing hospitalization he would agree to comply without much fuss.

Before taking the child to the hospital the parents should convince him that his health needs the attention of the kind doctors and nurses and he must go to the hospital to get well soon and return. Tell him that they would visit him at the hospital along with other members of the family. Never tell a falsehood to the child. When you have to leave him in the hospital bed, don't tell him that he should sleep and you will remain seated there. Don't give him a false hope that he would not be given the medicines. Convince him that he is ill and the treatment at the hospital is necessary for his quick recovery.

Legitimate Fear

As far as the legitimate fears of a child are concerned, the mentor should adopt a clever, thoughtful attitude towards them. Mention about dangerous situations to the child and discuss their remedies. Inform him about the bad consequences of negligence. Demonstrate to him the correct use of matches, gas and electrical gadgets and the dangers associated with these things.

Teach him the right way of crossing a busy road and acquaint him with the trafc rules for the pedestrians. Frankly mention to the child the dangers which might confront him in his daily life. Acquaint him with the safety measures and create in him the faith on himself and trust in Allah. He should be prepared to meet the challenges in his daily life, rather than getting scared of the dangers around him.

Another legitimate fear is the fear of death. But excessive fear of death turns into a psychic ailment. This fear takes away the spiritual calm and composure from a person. And blunts his physical capabilities. It is therefore necessary to take preventive measures against this type of fear. For sometime the child does not understand the meaning of death. It is better the mentor don't talk about this phenomenon at this stage. But sometimes the child learns about this at the death of someone close to him. It is quite possible the child might ask questions about death in such a situation.

If the child has reached the stage of understanding at that time, then the parents must reveal to him the truth. They must tell him that death is not anything special but it is a transition from the present world to another. In that world he will get reward for his good deeds and retribution for his evil deeds committed in this world. Everyone has to die one day. Allah says in the Holy The Holy Qur'an, '*All people will die*'. Death is not important but the actions in this life are important that the Judgment in the other world is made according to the actions of the person in this life.

Excessive thought of death is not good. It should not enter the realm of a lurking fear . This will be harmful.

Another positive aspect of fear is the fear of God and the fear of the Day of Judgment. These fears should not be so intense that they result in nervous tensions for the person. These fears encourage a person to do good deeds and stop him from evil acts. Therefore Allah says in the Holy Book:

> *"If you are among the faithful, fear not others and fear Me alone." (The Holy Qur'an, 3:175)*

Also the The Holy Qur'an describes the hardships and retributions of the Day of Judgment. Therefore a thoughtful and faithful mentor puts the idea of the rewards and punishments of the Hereafter in the impressionable minds of his charges.

It will be in place to remind that a good mentor should not all the time talk of the Heaven and the Hell and give an impression to the child that God is severe on His creations. But the mentor should acquaint the child more with the benevolence of Almighty Allah.

Play and Recreation

As breathing is necessary for the child, so is some exercise and play. At the preliminary and middle levels at the school the predominant activities of the children are sports, games and recreation. As they progress in their curricula, these activities are reduced.

Despite increasing load of scholastic work, the children have to take out some time for sports. Participating in outdoor games is an important physical activity that is essential for the good health of a child. Those children who don't take part in some outdoor games are generally not healthy. Islam is conscious of this natural prerequisite and therefore advises to keep the children physically free.

Imam Ja'far as-Sadiq says:

"Leave the child free to play till it is seven years old."[108] The Prophet of Islam says:

"Let them play; the earth is the pasture of the children!"[109]

Playing is a natural exercise for the child. This will make its limbs

---

[108] Wasail al-shiah, v 15, p. 193

[109] Majma az zawaid, v 8, p. 159

strong. The mental capabilities will sharpen and it will grow in strength. At the ground of play the child will be exposed to community living and sharing responsibilities with others.

The psychologists differ in their assessment of the importance of sports. We need not go into the details of their ndings. For us it is sufcient that play and physical exercise is an important aspect of the upbringing of a child.

The mentor therefore should not consider this only as an extra-curricular-activity. to be treated lightly. The child gets acquainted with the outside world while at play. He learns about performing tasks. He practices avoiding risks and also co-operating and co-ordinating with the members of his team. In team games he learns to respect the rights of others and learns about the rules of the games.

William Astern writes:

"Games are a source of developing the natural capabilities in the child. They are like an exercise for the future discipline and activities of the person."[110]

Alexi Maxim writes:

"Games provide to the child comprehension of life and a means of exercise to the body. Games help the child acquaint himself with the social norms. Play strengthens the child's feelings. The child in his play makes a house, builds a factory, takes an expedition to the North Pole, ies in the space and guards the borders of his country."

Anton Semonowich Makarno, a famous Russian expert on the subject of child-upbringing, says:

"If a person is smart in games and play in his childhood, he will reect the same quality in his life as he grows up. Good play is like doing good work. Every game requires the use of mental and physical capabilities. Observe a child at play and nd how he has formulated his

---

[110] Ruwan shinashi kudak, p. 331

strategy to succeed in that event. At play the feelings and sentiments of the child will be authentic. The elders should. Be observant of these."[111]

William Mc Dougal writes:

"Before nature manifests in the eld of activity, play reects the bent of the persons mind."[112]

Although, at play, the child is not performing any specic work, it is not less than performing a physical and mental work. During play the inclinations of the natural and personal capabilities will manifest themselves. While playing the character of the child takes shape for the bright future.

The guardians of children can be categorized in several ways:

There are those who consider playing with toys and games an unnecessary pastime and try their best to dissuade their children from taking part in any such activity.

There are others who are not against the children playing games and give them total freedom to select the toys and games of their choice to play.

The third category of guardians is those who don't attach any importance to game other than keeping the children occupied. They purchase toys and games without any other objective in view than providing some tools to the child to be fully occupied. The child plays with the toys, breaks them and throws them away when it is tired of them. The child also shows off his pretty toys and games to other children.

The fourth type of guardians are those who not only provide the means of play to the children but they keep a watch on the use of the material given to them. If the children come across any difculty in

---

[111] Ruwan shinashi kudak, p. 130

[112] Ruwan shinashi kudak, p. 332

using the newly acquired toys, they volunteer their assistance to solve the problem. Such guardians curb the problem solving instinct of the children and they get used to depending on the assistance of the elders in all matters.

Of the four categories of guardians, none completely measures up to the requirement of providing good learning experience to the child through play.

The best attitude that a guardian could adopt is that rst of all he should leave the child free that it plays in tune with its own nature and choice. Secondly he should provide a range of educational toys to the child. He should take care to select such toys and games that sharpen the thinking and creative capabilities of the child.

Another technical aspect the guardian has to keep in mind while selecting the toys and games is that the child should nd interest in constructive activities for self, the family and the society. It is a pity that most of the toys in the market have little educational value. For example, if one buys an electrically operated train or a car, the child will be busy looking at it all the day. But he will not learn anything that could be useful for him in the future.

The most useful toys are those which come in knocked-down condition and the child has to assemble them through trial and error method. For example, a collection of blocks which can be assembled into a building, incomplete paintings, jig-saw puzzles, stitching and embroidery material, carpentry tools etc

The mentor has to keep a watchful eye on the child at play that he can provide guidance to him at the right time. Watching children at play in itself is a very important aspect of training and upbringing.

A good teacher will provide the toys and games to the child and leave him alone to independently use them but will keep a subtle eye on the activity that the child is guided when he makes any mistake in the right use of the material.

For instance, when a toy car or toy train is given to the child, he is asked about the function of these machines. If the child replies that they are for moving men and materials from one place to another, then he is left alone to play with the toy. If the toy develops any defect during the use, leave it to the child to x it as far as possible.

The child may be guided in this regard that he develops self-condence in accomplishing the task. If you buy a doll for your daughter, it should not be in complete form. But you must guide her to prepare dresses for the doll. She will dress the doll, keep it clean, and play-act as if she is giving it a bath, changing the dress and giving it food. The child will sing a lullaby to make the doll sleep and wake it up to take it along. Emulating her elders, the child will teach good manners to the doll.

You will notice that the child puts into practice with the doll what she has heard from the elders. The child does most of the things in emulation of the acts of the parents and the elder siblings. The toys are useful when the child learns useful things of day-to-day life playing with them. The child must be encouraged to play with the toys rather that preserving them in a showcase and showing off to their playmates. There must be a proper place where the child should keep the toys after playing with them. The child must be encouraged to keep the place orderly and clean.

There should not be too many toys with the child at a time. This can tend to confuse the child and make it difcult to make a choice. The toys need not be expensive and very attractive.

The games for children can be categorized as:

Games which a child can play individually.

Games which two or more children can play together.

Educational games which give a llip to mental capability of the children. Outdoor games which provide growth to the physique of the children.

Games which promote in the children the capability of defense and attack. Games that promote the spirit of co-operation amongst the children.

In the beginning a child plays alone. It must be left alone to play, but an eye has to be kept on the child. The parents must make the right choice of the toys for the child. Sometimes the child wants to break the toy and assemble it again. The child must be allowed to do these experiments. Only when the child faces a difculty in these tasks, the elders should intervene.

After sometime the child starts liking the company of other children. Now he must be introduced to games where more than one child will play. The parents must encourage the child to play with other children.

At this stage too the parent should take care that the child is exposed to useful team games. The team games generally in vogue are football, volley-ball, basket-ball etc. Generally children play these games during their spare time at school and in their neighborhood. These games help development of the physique of the children, but they are highly competitive and make them temperamentally aggressive.

Children playing such games always have the thought of defeating their opponents. More aggressive than these games are boxing and wrestling. These games are a reminder of the primitive days of the human race. It is a pity that such games continue to be played.

Russel writes:

"Today's humanity, when compared with earlier epochs, has its biggest adversary in materialism, and therefore begs for more thoughtfulness and mutual co-operation in its ranks. Man doesn't need antagonism, resistance and hatred because these are things that sometimes overwhelm him and at other times he subdues them."[113]

It is of some concern that no thought is given to the matter and such

---

[113] Dar Tarbiat, p. 121

games that promote aggressive tendencies in the children are getting continuous patronage and encouragement. It would be better if the management of schools and colleges give a serious thought to this matter and consult experts to introduce useful games for children.

The concluding point in this discussion is that although play is essential for the growth of the children, the timing of the games must be restricted. A capable mentor schedules for play in such a manner that the child automatically reverts to constructive activities immediately thereafter. Such mentors don't allow the child to excessively involve in play.

'Ali, The Commander of the Faithful, says:

"One addicted to play will not be successful."[114] Russel writes about this:

"It is a sign of the decline of social values when we judge a person on his prociency at games. We have not understood that to live in the modern and complicated world there is need for thoughtfulness and knowledge."[115]

One drawback of team games is that they might create in the children the feelings of jealousy and conict. In such situations the mentor must intervene and sort out the dispute to the satisfaction of all concerned.

Sometimes parents get involved in the conicts between children. Without going into the causes of the conict they take sides with their own child and the matter goes out of hands. Such thoughtless attitude gives the child the feeling that he can get away with any misdemeanor on his part.

---

[114] Gharar al hukm, p. 854

[115] Dar Tarbiat, p. 142

Conceit or Pride

Conceit and boastfulness is present in every individual to a lesser or greater extent. Every person will have a desire to project himself by performing some feat or other. He intends to attract the attention of others around him through these actions. In a child these tendencies start manifesting themselves when it is about a year old.

The child wants to move around and attract the attention of others through its antics. It will repeat acts that make the parents and others happy. It will be pleased at the reaction of the parents and feels a subtle pride at its success in making them happy. The child sometimes indicates its satisfaction through gestures as if to assert its importance.

Pride in itself is not a negative trait. In fact, this feeling spurs an individual to strive for greater achievement with a competitive spirit. The child works hard to get a higher grade in his class. He tries to develop skills at elocution or become a skilled painter. It is this desire in the child to compete that proves the harbinger of the great poets, artists, authors and scientists of the future.

The presence of this trait of pride in children need not be a cause for worry. But the important thing is that it must be gainfully exploited to the advantage of the child. If it is guided in the right direction there can be salutary results. In the initial stages the child cannot distinguish between good and bad. It observes the reactions of the parents to decide at its actions and to arrive at a conclusion. A careful mentor will encourage the child's desirable actions by expressing happiness at them. The mentor can encourage good manners in a child by indicating his displeasure at its undesirable actions.

Some thoughtless parents, out of their love for the child, shower excessive adulation and praise without giving a thought as to whether the actions of the child are desirable or not. They thus lay the foundations of bad manners in the child inadvertently. In their adulation for the child they exaggerate its good qualities and keep praising the child at the drop of a hat.

There is every probability of such a child becoming conceited and progressively he becomes egotistic and arrogant. He will start expecting others' adulation as he does from his parents. When the child fails in getting the desired response, he becomes distraught. He develops rancor towards people and might even go to the extent of thinking of causing harm to them at a later stage.

The parents should bear in mind that they have to groom the thinking of the child to guide him on the path of righteousness. Then will come the stage that the parents divert the child's mind towards God. Now on, if any of the child's action is found incorrect, instead of saying that dad doesn't approve of it, they should tell him that God will not approve of it.

Taqleed or Emulation

The instinct to emulate is the strongest characteristic of human nature. This too is a very useful and valuable trait. This helps the child to progress with its learning process like eating, dressing, speaking and other societal happenings in the environment.

The human being is a natural mimic and keeps doing it throughout his life but children till the age of around ve years do this more. For a long time the faculties of the child are not so developed that it is not able to decide the course of action by itself. In this period it emulates what the parents and others do in front of him.

The child hears the word "water" from its parents and tries to repeat it himself. Then it gives attention to the meaning of the word and uses the word at appropriate time. A girl observes her mother cleaning the room and washing the clothes. She too tries to do the same chores. She sees that the mother exercises care while handling re, she sees that the mother washes the fruits prior to peeling and eating them.

The child too emulates these habits. She observes that the parents and her elder siblings are arranging things properly in the house. She too tries to copy them in these activities. She notices that her parents are polite in their talk with others, she too cultivates good manners.

She nds that the parents and her siblings are aiding each other in doing household work. She too tries to give a helping hand.

When she sees that the parents cross the roads carefully at pedestrian-zebra-crossing, she too learns to do this. When the son sees his father gardening in the backyard or does some repair work at the house, he too tries to learn the tasks. In the beginning he tries to do these things in play but with the passage of time he becomes procient. Some of them become so adept that they take the activity as a profession.

The upbringing and training of the child is better achieved by setting an example for him rather than through precept. Emulation of the actions of the elders is an automatic phenomenon in the children and they needn't necessarily be told to perform these actions. If a parent is boorish, impolite and impertinent the child will follow in his footsteps. When a mother is nagging, shrewish and insensible then there is every likelihood of the child going after her.

A mentor who is a liar, cowardly and dishonest person cannot expect to make his subject a truthful, bold and honest individual. The children don't pay much heed to the lecturing of the elders. They rather prefer to emulate their actions. It is therefore imperative to promote the habit of emulation in the children. Care has to be exercised to see that the elders perform such actions in the company of children that they grow into ideal individuals. For the love of their children the parents must reform their own habits to provide an ideal image for them. The parents should always bear in their mind that it is very difcult to stop the children from emulating their own habits, good or bad.

The Commander of the Faithful, 'Ali, says:

"If you wish to reform others then reform yourself rst. It is a major failing that you stand up to correct

others while you yourselves are having aberrations which need reform."[116] The Holy Prophet told to Abu Dharr:

"Allah will give noble and virtuous children and grand children to pious parents."[117]

A responsible mentor will not remain indifferent to the type of friends the child has. The children have very impressionable minds and they tend to readily emulate the habits of their friends. It is therefore very important to take care of the type of company the children keep.

Sometimes when the children witness acts of violence on the cinema or television screen they may develop a tendency for perpetrating such acts. You must be reading about such acts of delinquency by children in the newspapers and the motivation for these acts mostly is the scenes of murder and mayhem presented on cinema and television. In such circumstances is it proper to expose the children to these media without any control?

---

[116] Ghara al-hukm, p. 278

[117] Makarim al akhlaq, p. 546

Search for the Truth

When a new-born arrives it is not aware of the world around him. He cannot distinguish one thing from another. He will not be able to identify faces, colors and persons. It will be able to take impression from the faces and the sounds around him, but he will not be able to comprehend and identify one from another.

But, from this point only he will start developing the faculty of identifying persons and things. He will searchingly look from side to side and will give the expression of pleasant surprise seeing faces around him. Through the use of his senses and the instinct to learn, the child will continuously acquire knowledge about the surroundings.

Allah says in the Holy The Holy Qur'an:

> *"Allah has delivered you from the wombs of your mothers in a condition that you knew nothing. He has given to you ears, eyes and the heart that you identify Allah's bounties and become grateful." (The Holy Qur'an, 16:78)*

After some time of birth the child starts to give attention to the world around him. He holds things with his hands, moves them and throws them down. Sometimes he tries to put things in his mouth. He gets attracted in the direction of sounds in his environment.

He observes the action of the persons around him with his eyes. In this manner the child satiates his instinct to search for the truth. Allah has provided the faculty of search and adventure to human beings that they try to unravel the mysteries of the universe.

The child has this instinct in him and it starts getting manifested from his very early days. The parents can guide and encourage this instinct in children and they can also curb it with their negative actions. If the parents provide to the child aids that promote the desire to search and give him freedom to nd out about them, he can make steady progress in his knowledge.

This can be the vanguard for the scientic research and inventions in the future. But if the parents are oblivious to the inner feelings of the child and curb his desire to nd out about things, prevent him from making experiments, then the spirit to search in him will be suppressed.

The more critical stage in the life of the child is when he starts asking questions about things. The age of two years and above is the age when the child will have lots of questions to ask. The child asks the parents whether he will become a mother or a father? Why dad goes away for a time from the house every day? Why a stone is hard and the water is soft? I don't like Granny, Why should I go to her house? Why shouldn't I play in the rain? Why sh don't die in water? Why do you pray ve times a day? What is Namaz/*salah* (prayer)?

Where does the Sun go in the nights? From where does the rain and snow come? What are the stars, who made them? What is the use of the sh and the ies? When the grandpa died, why was he buried in the ground? Where has he gone? When will he return? What is death? More or less all the children ask such questions. As they grow they will have different types of questions to ask. Intelligent children will ask more questions and diverse questions. As their knowledge increases, they start asking more intricate questions. The child tries to learn about the things around him by asking questions.

It wishes to benet from the knowledge and experience of others. The urge to search and explore is the most vital instinct of the human being that enables him to scale heights in all elds of activity. Man has been able to unravel the mysteries of the universe with dauntless effort at research and exploration. The parents who are aware that the instinct in the child to nd out about things needs to be promoted to help him make progress in his knowledge for future progress will extend their full support and attention to him during the early years.

Some parents consider the childish question as unnecessary and a waste of time. They even go to the extent of snubbing the child to stop him from asking such questions. They tell them, "Sonny Don't ask too many questions. When you grow up you will yourself learn about what you are asking now!" Such parents silence the most valuable instinct in the child by their unwillingness to entertain the questions. They unwittingly become the cause of slowing down the urge for knowledge in the child. At a later stage they complain that their child is not able to cope with the study of science and other disciplines.

Some parents, to please the children, do reply to their questions but they never bother to ensure the veracity of the answers. Their only momentary purpose is to quiet the child with some answer. When the child learns later on that the parent had given to him a wrong information, he would feel bad about it. It may also make the child suspicious about others.

Thoughtful and responsible parents appreciate their duty to provide the right answers to the childrens' questions and encourage their instinct to nd out about nature of things around them. They prepare themselves about this task by visualizing the questions the child might ask and explore the possible replies to the queries.

They never tell anything to the child that is contrary to the truth. If at times they don't have the right answer to the child's question, they own their inability and try to nd the right answer to be given later on. This way they train the child to be frank when he himself is faced with a similar situation. Some parents go into unnecessary detail while answering a child's question. This too is not desirable Experience tells that a child doesn't want to listen to long-winded answers.

Although it wants a reply to the question, long talks will make it tired. The parents must encourage the habit of debate and discussion in the children as they grow up. Where necessary they must be assisted to experiment. A child is a thinking human being, provide impetus to its thinking process that the latent capabilities are put into use and prepare itself for the future.

'Ali, The Commander of the Faithful, says:

"One who asks questions in his childhood, will be capable of replying to questions when he is grown up."[118]

"The child's heart is like the soft soil. Whatever you put into it will be accepted."[119] A lady writes in her letter thus:

"One evening Dad came home and narrated a riddle to me. He also said that his friends were unable to solve that riddle. Everyone at home slept but I was determined to unravel the riddle. I thought over it for a long while and ultimately I got the solution. I was so excited that I woke up Dad from his sleep. He expressed his happiness over my effort to solve the riddle. He always encouraged me to sharpen my intellect. He has prepared me well to face the problems of life wisely."

---

[118] Gharar al hukm, p. 645

[119] Gharar al hukm, p. 302

Self-Confidence

The life of a human being is full of struggle, challenges and competition. Every human comes across thousands of challenges and difculties in the lifetime. To live he will have to ght with the powers of the elements unwillingly and has to overpower them. He has to contend with different ailments and their causes. In practical life he is successful who has a big heart, tall courage and strong will. The good or ill luck of a person depends rather on his own self. The success of all the great persons in the world is because of their own condence, will power and tireless efforts.

The great and weighty persons are never cowed down by hardships. They have self-condence and Faith in Allah that takes them through all the vicissitudes of life. They are able to accomplish tasks which seem impossible to others. They are not like a straw in the vast ocean which keeps oating on the surface of the water with the wind.

But they are like the powerful swimmer who has strong arms and a will and faith in the Almighty Allah that give them the ability to swim against the direction of the wind. These are the persons who are capable of determining the shape of things to come in the world. Islam too says that the temporal and spiritual success of a person depends on his own actions and determination. The Holy The Holy Qur'an says:

> *"Whatever man has is the result of his own efforts and he will soon see his endeavor (in full form)." (The Holy Qur'an, 53:39-40)*

The Commander of the Faithful, 'Ali, says:
"The price of every individual is equal to his courage."[120]

A person who has patience and self-condence will not look to others for the solution of his problems. He in fact jumps into the arena with complete faith in himself and never gives up till he achieves his goal.

Imam Ja'far as-Sadiq says:
"The secret of the respect and greatness of a Mu'min (a pious person) is that he does not crave for things in others' hands."[121]

Imam Sajjad says:
"All the virtues are there in the fact that a person does not sit waiting for assistance from others."[122]

But people who lack self-condence don't trust on their own capabilities. They consider themselves weak and lowly. They are scared of facing the hardships of life. They will shirk from responsibilities. They make easy tasks difcult by negative thoughts and hopelessness. They spend their lives in despondency and dejection.

Now that the importance of patience and self-condence is established, it will not be out of place to remind that the basis of these characteristics is inherent in the nature of every human being. But they need to be nurtured and trained. The ideal and most pertinent

---

[120] Nahj al balagha, v 2, p. 163

[121] Usul al-Ka, v2, p. 148

[122] Usul al-Ka, v2, p. 148

period of this training is the very childhood of the person.

The rudiments of patience and assurance get manifested from the childhood of every individual. The characteristics contrary to these, namely: impatience and lack of condence, dependence on others too start developing because of faulty training by the parents. The parents have to train their children with care that they grow into useful individuals.

Imam Zain al Abidin says:

"Train your children in such a way that they bring respect and eminence to you."[123]

From the age of four years to the age of eight years is the best period for the shaping of the personality and poise in an individual. In this period the child will be inclined towards patience and forbearance and prepares himself to face the hardships. Although the child will be aware of its weakness and the need for dependence on a superior, it will also have the elements of patience and poise in its nature. It wishes to fulll its needs. It feels elated at performing new tasks. You must have heard the children uttering these words:

- See, what I am doing?
- Did you see how I jumped?
- Look, I can wear my own dress.
- I shall put on the shoe myself
- I shall drink water from the tumbler
- I want to eat the food with my own hands.
- I don't want you to pour the tea for me.
- Look at the beautiful picture I have drawn.
- I want to climb on the tree.

---

[123] Tuhaf al uqul, p. 269

The child insists that he would spend the money in his pocket the way he wants. He wants to arrange his toys himself. Sometimes he becomes stubborn with the parents to get his way. Sometimes the child wants to give a helping hand to the parents at the chores. The little daughter tries to wash utensils and clothes with her mother. She wants to cook food and arrange the dining table.

The little son tries to spruce up the garden. He wants to draw pictures, write letters and go out shopping with the father. He will insist that he would select his own dress and footwear. While walking on the road he shows his preference sometimes to walk ahead of the parents and at others he prefers to trail behind them. He likes to take part in the arrangement of the furniture in the house. He refuses to eat certain type of foods. With such acts the child demonstrates his individuality. To the maximum possible extent the child tries not to be dependent on others.

The personality of the child will be a reection of the parents' disposition. The parents should give a degree of independence to the child that he progresses with self-condence. They should express pleasure and appreciation when the child achieves something new. They should assign to him tasks that are to his liking and within his ken. With guidance and encouragement hone his capabilities. The child will progressively gain in condence.

A psychologist writes:

"A person notices a little sherman efciently catching sh. He was getting big catches. The man was surprised. He praised the skill of the young sherman. The boy thanked him for the praise and said, 'There is nothing surprising in my skill at shing because I have been doing it ever since I was very small'. The person asked him, ' But, what is your age?' He replied, ' six years!' "

If the parents had not encouraged him and, to the contrary, dissuaded him from starting to do the job from an early age he wouldn't have been able to acquire such good skill. The parents who adore and adulate their children very much, inadvertently make them overly dependent on themselves. They don't allow the children to do any tasks. They try to do every small thing for the children. They make all the decision for the children themselves.

A large number of parents don't give any attention to the need for creating self-condence in the children. They express unhappiness over the mistakes of the children if they attempt to do some task themselves. They don't like the child innovating and discourage him at every step.

My dear parents Our children anyway have to grow up They too have to shoulder responsibilities in the future. You have to respond positively to the child's nature to be independent. The desire for independence is not a fault. This independence is the manifestation of the desire to achieve excellence with one's own efforts. You must ensure that the child is able to exercise his independence judiciously. You should not insist that you should make decisions for him when he can as well make them himself. You must explain the pros and cons to the child and allow him to make his own decision.

If the child starts to do something and gives it up half way, don't put him to shame with thoughtless interference. Leave the matter to him.

If your daughter wishes to cook the food herself, then give her guidance to do the task. Don't interfere while she is at the task. What is the harm if she spoils a dish once. Don't be critical of her skill at cooking. Do you realize the hurt caused to the child's psyche at such criticisms.

One lady writes:

"Whatever I tried to do in my childhood, I received rebukes—you broke the delicate china, you have put excessive salt in the dish, you have used more water than the recipe required. What do you know about sweeping the oor? Don't talk in the presence of guests… and hundreds of more such rebukes

Self-Confidence

While cooking I used to taste the dish lest there is excessive salt and water in the preparation. Even then I used to be always at the receiving end. This is the reason I could not develop condence in my capabilities. I started considering myself weak and insignicant. I am very unhappy with inferiority complex and lack of condence. I am in-charge of addressing a weekly meeting (*majlis*). Every time I stir out for the task I go with a disturbed mind...

I start doubting that I might not be able to handle the function properly. "My heart will be autter. I feel that I might not be able to deliver the talk properly. Many a time I remember a lot of points for the talk that I had also included in some past meetings. Even then I lack condence. I start wishing that this responsibility was not entrusted to me. Whatever work I do, I start to get the feeling of reluctance. Half way through any work I start wishing that this task was taken away from me. I tried hard to banish this lack of condence on myself but I have always failed."

Another lady writes:

"From my childhood mother tried to help me with my work. She never allowed me to do anything alone. In time I got used to the prop and depending on others became a part of my nature. I was not able to use my condence and capability to tackle problems. I always needed help from Mom and others at home. The dependence on others went to the extent that even for a trivial task I needed support of others. I had a feeling that I am incapable of doing anything on my own."

It must be mentioned at this stage that some children, to display their individuality accede to wrong actions. For example, they may mutilate the owers and pull out branches of shrubs, harm birds and dogs and cats. Harm others and pull the hair of the sisters. At such times the parents can't keep quiet without interfering. But they must bear in their minds that when the child does such things, he doesn't have rancor or hate towards anyone. He is just trying to assert his individuality. The best way of preventing him from such acts is to tacitly divert his attention to other things. Make him busy with some game or gainful task.

Independence

There are plenty of parents who think that restricting or denying any freedom to the children is good upbringing. They think that the children are incapable of distinguishing between good and bad. They don't have enough wisdom and if they are given some independence, they might go astray. Such parents start thinking for the child and make all the decisions for him.

They try to keep control over the child's eating, playing and other activities. They want to model the child's life according to their own thinking. They believe that the child doesn't have any right to independence and freedom. He should not do anything without the express permission of the parents.

Whatever the parents decide, the child must do implicitly without a whimper. Whatever the parents decide is wrong, the child must stop doing without any complaint. The children have no say in the plan of upbringing charted by such parents. Earlier, most families used to follow this policy for upbringing their children. They used to bring up the children with a iron hand. Even these days there are families that follow this practice of their forbears.

Although such has been the practice in the past, and is still followed by some families, it is not a desirable trend. It has many drawbacks and lacunae. There is always a possibility that with such training the children might remain comfortable, quiet and obedient to the parents. But they grow into timid persons devoid of self-condence. Their inventive and innovative instincts will become dormant. They will not have the courage to take up important and difcult tasks in hand. They are also not capable of becoming leaders.

But they will be habituated of taking orders and bearing ill treatment stoically. When they grow up, they are not able to overcome this defect easily. They carry a hitch in their psyche that might later on be the cause of several psychological ailments. It is also possible that such persons develop sadistic tendencies and become tyrannical with their children and others.

Many intellectuals and psychologists have started a campaign against this cruel practice of upbringing and are advocating total freedom for the children. They advise the parents to leave the children free to act according to their own desire and liking. They say that the child should be free to do anything that he desires, although it may not be the right thing in your eyes. This way the child will grow with an independent mind.

The famous psychologist Sigmund Freud believes in this method and has many followers in the East and the West. Lot of parents too followed this method in upbringing their children. They have given total freedom to their children and do not order them around. But this practice too is not totally right. It has several drawbacks. The children brought up this way don't believe in any restriction for doing what they decide to do. Such children generally will be selsh, excitable and of impudent nature. They think that others don't have any rights. They usurp others rights and privileges. They unnecessarily trouble their brothers and sisters. Such children tend to become a nuisance to their neighbors and others.

Independence

Because their desires are driven by total independence, they commit excesses towards others. Their expectations reach such a level that they will nd it difcult to fulll them. When such children grow into adults they expect others to obey them without any complaint. They don't want to be controlled by anyone else. When they notice that they are unable to get their way with others, then they become heart-broken

After having faced rebuffs in the society they become reclusive, or, to take revenge against their defeats they devise stratagems for tyranny and dangerous acts. Unrestricted freedom sometimes becomes hazardous too. Sometimes a child wishes to run dangerously on the road or to touch the live electrical wire. Thus, the two methods of upbringing, one that gives no freedom to the child and the other which

recommends total freedom, are both fraught with glaring faults. The best path to follow in the matter of the upbringing of the child is to give him selective freedom.

Allah has endowed the human beings with different instincts and feelings that go to make the nature of a person. Some of these instincts are love, hate, bravery, fear etc. These are intrinsic feelings and notions endowed by Allah to all human beings for tackling the problems that confront them. These instincts go to make the individual's personality. In a free environment these instincts keep growing.

Fear is for escape from dangers. Anger helps in deciding to attack the adversary. Diligence is required for acquiring learning. A person who does not have the instinct of fear and anger in his nature will be an inferior person. It is not right to suppress these instincts in a child. In an atmosphere of freedom a child can make use of these instincts to advantage.

The Religion of Islam gives particular attention to the need for freedom. A few traditions are quoted here. 'Ali said:

"Don't become slave to others, Allah has given birth to you as a free person."[124] Imam Ja'far as-Sadiq said:

"A person who has the following ve qualities will be a successful person: First: Faith, Second: Wisdom, Third: Morals, Fourth: Freedom, Fifth: Good behavior."

The Prophet of Islam said:

"The child is a ruler till he is seven years old, seven to fourteen years he is a subject and after fourteen years he is the deputy and adviser for his parents."[125]

But total freedom is not possible in the society. For one person's freedom, the freedom of others in the society cannot be compromised. The child must be made to understand early in life that without any restrictions one cannot live in the society.

Others too have some rights and privileges. For example: a child wants to play. Play is good for his training He must have freedom to play games that suit his temperament. But while playing the child should be aware of the rights of others. He should exercise care that property of the neighbors is not damaged, the window-panes of buildings in the neighborhood are not broken. Therefore, he does have the freedom to play but this freedom is having some restrictions.

The child can exercise his instinct to get angry. He can defend himself by showing anger at proper time. But in the exercise of his anger he does not have the freedom to damage the property around him, cause some injury to others or heap insults at them.

The parents should devise a strategy for the upbringing of the child keeping in consideration his age, intelligence, strength and feelings. They should put his actions in two categories:

---

[124] Bihar al-anwar, v77, p.214

[125] Wasail al-shiah, v 15, p. 195

1. The actions that is desirable for him.
2. The actions that are taboo for him.

They should determine the limit for each type of action. Then they should give total freedom to the child for the desirable activity so that he fully exercises his instincts in performing these activities without any restriction. The child should be free to think and act. Not only the child should be given total freedom, but also on occasion he must be guided, if so required. But the acts which are taboo for the child, he should be strictly prevented from doing them.

If this attitude is adopted, neither will the freedom of the child be curbed nor his capabilities hindered. He will have the right amount of freedom and control to ensure that his instincts are utilized gainfully.

The parents should carefully determine the right and wrong acts that the child might do. The acts which are harmful to the family, which might cause harm to the persons or property, which are against the norms of *Shariah* and the law should be black-listed and the child should be strictly prevented from perpetrating them. For the right acts the child should be given total freedom. In performance of these good acts the child should be allowed to use his own thinking and intuition.

The rules of behavior should be determined keeping in view the strength of his body and mind, his thinking capacity. Care should be taken to set rules which are not harsh on the child.

The parents should be rm in their pronouncements to the child, "You can do this." "You must not do this."

The parents should keep aside unnecessary sentiments and emotions. They should abstain from doubts and suspicions so that the child understands its responsibilities and will not have any hesitation in fullling his duties.

Imam Hasan al Askari says:

"When a child disobeys his parents, and is impertinent to them, he will grow into an adult who is rebellious and insubordinate."[126]

The parents must both co-ordinate with one another to abstain from differences of opinion while dealing with the child. The differences amongst the parents can create doubts in the mind of the child.

---

[126] Bihar al-anwar, v78, p. 374

Stubbornness

Every child will have a degree of stubbornness in its nature that becomes evident from the age of two years. A stubborn child generally insists to get things done his way. Whenever he finds some resistance from others, he will have recourse to crying and shouting. It will roll on the ground and hit its head against the walls.

The child may even refuse to have food. It will throw the crockery and sometimes even become aggressive and hit the other members of the family. This habit of stubbornness, if it persists, is also noticed in grown up youth.

Generally the parents complain about this aberration in their children and keep searching a solution to the problem. It is the common experience that the parents have access to one of the two methods, mentioned here, to overcome the problem:

Firstly: Some parents are of opinion that a tough attitude should be taken, if the child is stubborn, by refusing to accede to his demands. These parents say that the child has become very assertive and they need to be firm in denying its wishes. They try to correct the child by being strict and go to the extent of punishing and beating him.

They try to impose their own wishes on the child. The behavior of such parents is tantamount to tit-for-tat attitude. This approach is not desirable even if they have momentarily quietened the child by being strict. To the contrary they cause grave harm to the psyche of the child with their strict attitude.

Two years is the age of the onset of self-determination and condence in a child. The obstinate behavior of the child is the assertion of its nature of independence. At this tender age the child is not capable of controlling its wishes and imagining the consequences of fullling them.

It makes up its mind and wants the things done accordingly. If the parents deny him his wishes, they would be hurting the child's psyche. Such children might grow into calm individuals but they will be devoid of the trait of condence and determination.

When a child notices that nobody is concerned about its wishes and are preventing him by force from having his way, then he will become dejected and disappointed. This condition of unrest and frustration becomes a part of his nature. There can also be the possibility of his becoming rebellious as he grows up and indulges in extreme acts like tyranny and murder as an expression of his extreme feelings of hurt.

Secondly: Some experts on the subject of upbringing believe that, to the extent possible, the child's wishes should be satised. He must be allowed to do what he wishes to. They feel that the child should be given a degree of independence. They believe that as the child grows up, it will stop being stubborn. But this method of handling the children too has its own aws.

There are certain acts that can be harmful to the child and others around him, if he is allowed to do them. The elders closing their eyes to such acts of the child is not being wise. Imagine a three-year-old trying to scale a ladder unhindered. The possibility of his falling and maiming himself for life will always be there. The child might try to light the oven unattended and consequently cause a big re. The child may get into its head to bodily harm other children around him. The elders always have to prevent the child from doing such things.

The child who is free to do what he likes, and nds acceptance for these acts, with unruly behavior will in stages become a selsh and dictatorial individual. He expects that people will accept his point of view without complaint. He has not met with any denial of his wishes in the childhood and expects the same attitude from others when he has grown up. But in practice this is not the case. People can differ with his points of view. After facing many such denials he gets frustrated and becomes reclusive. He will consider himself a defeated person and thinks that others are unreasonable.

Islam considers stubbornness as a negative trait in an individual as several traditions can be quoted in this regard:

For instance, 'Ali, The Commander of the Faithful, says:

"Stubbornness is the cause of evil."[127]

"Brazenness (or stubbornness) causes harm to the human intelligence."[128]

"Stubbornness is the cause of conict and enmity."[129]

"Stubbornness harms a person the most in this world and Hereafter."[130]

The best attitude is one of moderation. The parents who adopt this way of upbringing their children don't consider the stubbornness of the child as an aberration and are aware that it is the expression of his individuality. Instead of curbing this instinct, they use is for the training and upbringing of the child.

They carefully consider and analyze the demands and acts of the

---

[127] Ghirar al-hukm, p. 16

[128] Ghirar al-hukm, p. 17

[129] Ghirar al-hukm, p. 18

[130] Ghirar al-hukm, p. 104

child. They give freedom to the child for his acts that are harmless and thus encourage the growth of its mental capabilities. They become his friends and give him a helping hand in the performance of his actions.

Such children strengthen their determination to perform acts and give expression to their individualities. These children consider the parents as their friends and not persons who unnecessarily impede their actions.

But such parents assert constraint on the harmful acts of the children and don't mince words in advising the child to refrain from such acts. They clearly explain the reasons for stopping the child from such acts and divert its mind to some other useful activity.

Because the child has a good feeling towards the parents, who don't put too many restrictions on him, agrees to refrain from the act which they ask him not to do. But if sometimes the child persists with his demand for doing an undesirable act, .the parents have to put their foot down and prevent him from doing it. The child will then cool down after some time.

The child should be trained to realize that in life one cannot always be stubborn; the parents must exercise restraint while handling the children and should not take recourse to beating them. The child should not get the idea that the parents are tyrannical such children can turn rebellious with passage of time.

At the end of this discussion, it is in place to mention the following points for the consideration of the mentors:

1. As far as possible give freedom for action to the children. Don't interfere too much with their actions. Don't perpetually keep on telling them not to do things. When the child tries to climb over a chair or a shrub, you ask him not to do it He tries to peel a fruit; you stop him from doing it lest he cut his ngers He wants to light the water-heater, you prevent him from doing it, fearing he

might burn his hand He tries to pour decoction in a teacup, you stop him saying he might break the expensive China He plays inside the house, you say he is making too much of noise He stirs out into the lane, you fear he might be run over by a bicycle Then, what would you expect the little child to do He too has human feelings When you interfere too much with his acts, he might develop stubbornness. One reason for the trait of stubbornness in the children is excessive interference of the parents in their actions.

2. When a child becomes querulous, then try to nd the reason for this and nd a solution. The child will then calm down. If he is hungry, feed him. If he is tired, help him to sleep. If the child is disturbed with the environment, like a noisy television near him, or noisy visitors around, set the environment right for him.
3. Don't insult or upbraid the child that can make him more stubborn. 'Ali says: "Reprimand gives wind to the re of stubbornness."[131]
4. Sometimes the siblings commit excesses on a child and he nds no supporter. He will then become rebellious and stubborn. In such cases the parents must intervene.
5. If your child behaves stubbornly and you are unable to fathom the reason for this; then introspect whether his behavior is because of your own failing.

1. Ghirar al-hukm, p. 16
2. Ghirar al-hukm, p. 17

---

[131] Tuhaf al-uqul, p. 80

Work and Performance of Duties

Work and efforts to achieve are the basis of human life. Through work man acquires the basic amenities of food, clothing and shelter these needs are fullled by making tireless efforts throughout ones life.

The growth of industries and mind-boggling inventions are all the results of continuous research and development activity of human beings. It is sheer hard work and knowledge that gave birth to the civilizations in the world. It is the collective greatness of the people of a country that they have a prominent place in the comity of nations.

The prosperity of any country is a direct reection of the hard efforts put in by the people of that nation. If the people of a country are lazy and compulsive malingerers, that country will lag behind others in all elds of activity. Such countries will not be prosperous. Such nations will not be productive and will always remain in the morass of backwardness.

Similarly the progress of every individual too will depend on his knowledge, skills and sincerity of efforts. The world is a place for hard work and toil. It has no place for people who shirk and avoid their duties.

Allah says in the Holy Book:

"Whatever man has got is the result of his striving." (The Holy Qur'an, 53:39)

The Prophet of Islam says:
"Accursed is one who puts his burden on others."[132] The Prophet also said:
"Prayer has seventy aspects and the most excellent is the toil to obtain honest livelihood."[133] Imam Ja'far as-Sadiq says:
"Convey my greetings to my friends and exhort them to remain pious and prepare themselves for the Day of Reckoning. By Allah I ask you do such things, which I myself with hard toil After morning prayers, stir out early for work and acquire honest livelihood. Allah will then provide you food and succour."[134]

Imam Muhammad Baqir says:
"I don't like the person who is lazy in performing his worldly duties. A person who is slow in this life will also be slow Hereafter."[135]

Imam Ja'far as-Sadiq says:
"A person who toils to provide sustenance to his family will get the reward equivalent to a *jihad*."[136]

Imam as-Sadiq also said:
"The farmers are depositories for men. They sow good seeds and Allah helps them grow. On the Day of Judgment the farmers will have an excellent place. They will be addressed with the sobriquet of

---

[132] Usul al-Ka, v5, p. 73

[133] Usul al-Ka, v5, p. 78

[134] Usul al-Ka, v5, p. 78

[135] Usul al-Ka, v5, p. 85

[136] Usul al-Ka, v5, p. 88

mubarakain—the blessed ones."[137]

Every human being derives benet from the efforts and work of others. The human beings are symbiotic and cannot live in seclusion. It is therefore the duty of every individual to make his best efforts for his own sustenance and for other fellow beings. The laborers therefore can be rated as the best of human beings. Those who have the strength to work but depend on the toil of others will be deprived of the Blessings of Allah.

The parents, who wish to make their children grow into obedient and useful citizens, and also they want to contribute to the progress of their nation, must initiate the children to do some useful work early in life. They should train the children in such a way that they develop aptitude for work very early.

This way they will be able to inculcate the spirit of dignity of labor in the children. Such persons will not deem any work below their dignity. Lot of parents don't give attention to this very important aspect of the training of their children. They keep doing many simple things for the child that he could himself do without any difculty.

With this attitude they don't create a sense of responsibility in the child. They presume that this way they are serving the child. To the contrary it can be a disservice to the child and the society at large. With their attitude they create drones who will shirk work as they grow up. The child must be encouraged and helped to do work that suits his age and physical capability. This way the habit of work will be created in the child and he will enjoy working.

The ignorant parents, who do every small work for the child, are not absolving themselves from the duty of training the child and creating lazy and useless members for the society.

Responsible and thoughtful parents keep in mind the child's age,

---

[137] Usul al-Ka, v5, p. 201

physical strength and his mental capability into and encourage him to perform tasks that are within his ken. For example, a child of three years is asked to put on the socks himself, put on the shorts himself or to fetch things like the salt seller etc.

As the child grows up, bigger tasks are entrusted to him, like making his own bed, setting the dining table, washing the dishes, cleaning and swabbing the oors etc. The children are also encouraged to look after their younger siblings; tend the garden at home and attend on the pets. Then they are trained to go shopping for grocery and other small needs for the household.

As the child grows, he can be initiated into doing more difcult tasks. In this regard there are some important factors that the parents must keep in mind:

1. Keeping in view the age and physique of the child, they must entrust to him work that suits his aptitude. Sometimes the child himself expresses his wish to do certain tasks. These tasks generally pertain to his personal needs. He must be allowed to do these tasks or else he will get used to depending on others for every small thing.
2. The child's physical strength and courage should always be kept in mind and tasks beyond his capacity should not be entrusted to him. Otherwise the child might get the feeling of ennui and refuse to do any work later on. If the work is tiring for the child, he might show hostility towards such tasks.
3. Try to explain the task to the child while entrusting it to him. Impress on him that things don't happen by themselves at home. The father works hard to run the household. The mother too works hard on the chores at home. The child too must extend his support in running the household by doing tasks that he is capable of. At these times the parents must refrain from using

force in making the child work. The child must enjoy doing small tasks at home and should not be working under duress.

4. If possible, allow the child to select the responsibilities and work of his choice. For example, he may be given the choice either to wash dishes at home or do oor swabbing.
5. The quantum and limits of the works should be properly explained to the child. This will make him aware of his responsibility and there will not be the likelihood of his going beyond his specied limits.
6. The children who have special aptitude, should be entrusted with specic tasks. For example, one child may be told to ensure that there should always be fresh salads on the table at meal times. He should take care of replenishing stocks of fresh salads and other groceries like soaps, tooth paste, detergents etc.
7. Efforts must be made to entrust such tasks to the child that are to his liking and will do them willingly. But in certain cases the child may be required to do things that are not liked by him. The child must be encouraged to perform some tasks of this nature, which will be a good training for him. 'Ali says, "Allocate tasks to the persons at home. When they understand their individual responsibility they will not think that the task has to be performed by someone else."[138]
8. If you have many children at home, be just in allocating work to them equitably.
9. To encourage the children to do tasks at home, participate with them. The children feel important when they see the parents working with them.
10. If there is total understanding between the parents in the performance of household chores, then they can be an excellent

---

[138] Gharar al hukm, p. 124

example for the children to emulate. The children in such homes will be willing to take up responsibilities.
11. When the children are grown up and capable of taking up economically benecial tasks, then the parents must arrange for them such activities. This way, they will be busy and also supplement the family's income. Impress on them that there is no embarrassment in doing any work and , to the contrary, it is a matter of pride.

However, the children should not be put to too much pressure of work. They must be provided with ample opportunities and time for play and recreation. It is not right to think that because the parents are afuent there is no need for their children to work. This way the children might turn into gallivants, and lazy individuals.

In the end we wish to remind that the foundation for the will to work is laid in the very childhood of an individual so that it becomes the second nature of the person. Otherwise, breaking a person into work at a later stage will be a very difcult task. Responsible parents should not neglect this very critical aspect of training for their children.

A lady writes thus in her memoirs:

"I am a very lazy, defeatist and stubborn person. I am always restless and under pressure of imaginary fears. I have inammation of my intestines. I have no inclination to do any work. Doing anything is very difcult for me. I am fed up of doing household chores and cooking. This is the reason that I am always having differences with my spouse and mother-in-law.

The cause of all this misfortune is my mother. She was a very kind, patient and courageous lady. But she never entrusted any work to me, perhaps, out of her love for me. She never entrusted any responsibility to me. She didn't want to tire me doing household chores. She never gave a thought to the fact that I would be required to run a house in the future for which I was not being trained. ."

Another lady writes in a letter:

"…. I am the eldest of the daughters of the family. I am totally satised with my life. I don't feel any shortcomings in my living standards. I am not of a jealous nature. I am kind and helpful to others. Jewelry and wealth have no particular signicance for me. I perform my responsibilities with dignity. I have no regrets for anything in life. I am living a clean, calm and peaceful life. I am thankful to my parents that it is all thanks to the upbringing they have given to me.

While entering the house my Dad used to call me to hand-over his shopping for keeping carefully. He used to give me his shirt for stitching the button or used to give his suit to be ironed. He used to appreciate my work and thank me. Once I stitched a new dress for him. He expressed his happiness and promised to buy a sewing machine for me.

After a few days he fullled his promise. He brought a good sewing machine for me. From that day I was responsible for the stitching and sewing work at home. My mother used to give me expensive cloth and used to say, ' have no fear of spoiling the material. If you spoil it once, you will learn to sew better in the future.'

Because of the reassuring attitude of my Mom my condence increased by leaps and bounds. I always tried to do the tasks carefully. I don't recall if I had ever spoilt the cloth !

I learnt everything with the loving support of my parents. I got used to taking responsibilities and doing my tasks efciently. It is my desire to give similar upbringing to my children.

Straightforwardness

Telling lies is a very abhorrent habit and is one of the major sins. All the races of the world condemn lying. The persons who lie are looked down upon. A person known to be a liar has no condence or respect of his compatriots. A noble and good person never tells lies. Islam has categorically condemned this bad habit.

Imam Muhammad al Baqir says:

"Lies are the cause of faithlessness."[139] Imam Ja'far as-Sadiq says:

" Isa said that who lies repeatedly will not be respected."[140] 'Ali has said:

"There is no action more inferior than telling lies."[141]

All the prophets of Allah and every reformer has invited people to say the truth. Truth is a natural instinct. Everyone likes the truth. Even a compulsive liar would always like to hear the truth. If a child is left to his own scruples, it is in his nature to tell the truth. It is the

---

[139] Usul al-Ka, v4, p. 32

[140] Usul al-Ka, v4, p. 33

[141] Mustadarak al-wasail, v2, p. 100

inuence of the external factors that make a person adopt the habit of telling lies.

A child is absolutely incapable of lying. In later life when he is exposed to circumstances that force him to lie, he might get into that bad habit. Any amount of sermonizing, reference of verses of the The Holy Qur'an and Traditions of the Infallibles may not have any effect on the person.

It is the duty of the parents that they ensure their children are truthful from childhood. They should carefully remove the causes of falsehood and inculcate truthfulness in their natures. They should not neglect to promote truthfulness in the children.

The parents who are interested in good upbringing of their children and feel their responsibility in this regard should consider the following facts:

1. The one thing that will have salutary effect on the child's upbringing is the atmosphere in the family. The child grows in this environment. He learns good manners from the parents and others in the house. If the atmosphere in the house is one of truth and correctness, the parents and others are treating each other correctly, then the child will follow suit.

To the contrary, if the atmosphere at home is one of falsehood, the parents lie to each other and the children; then the innocent children will pick up the same habits. The children whose ears get habituated to hearing lies uttered all around them, can never be expected to think in any other way. Some ignorant parents not only tell lies but also encourage their children too to tell lies for obtaining some momentary benet. The father remaining at home tells his son to tell a visitor that he is not home. When a child misses school the parent asks him to tell the teacher that he was not well.

Thus the habit of malingering is encouraged. There are hundreds of lies that are traded around the houses every day such parents are doing a grave injustice to their innocent and impressionable children. Telling lies is a sin and teaching children to lie is a greater sin

Therefore, the parents who wish their children to be truthful have no other way than being truthful themselves. It is just leading by example!

Russel writes:

"If you wish that your children don't get into lying habit, then the only method is to always tell the truth in their presence."[142]

I wish Russel had said, "Adopt truthfulness in the presence of children as also with everyone else !"The child's nature is affected with all falsehood, even if it is hidden.

Imam as-Sadiq says:

"Invite people to good without use of your tongue. People should see your piety, diligence, prayer and good deeds that are a role model for them."[143]

1. The child by nature does not lie. His natural instinct urges him to uphold the truth. He needs a very strong reason to tell a falsehood. If the parents get to the depth of the reason for the falsehood, and remove these reasons, the child will become truthful. One reason that makes a child lie is the fear of the parents admonishment.

When you ask him if he had broken the window pane, he would say, "No!" Remember, the reason for the child uttering a falsehood is his fear of the parents. Then he shifts the responsibility of the broken glass pane to some other person. If the parents are clever and thoughtful, the

---

[142] Dar tarbiat, p. 148

[143] Usul al-Ka, v 2, p. 780

reason for the child telling lies will never be there. There can always the possibility that the window glass was broken unintentionally.

Then there is no reason to reprimand the child. The parents need to tell the child softly to be more careful in the future.

In these circumstances the child doesn't deserve to be reprimanded or beaten that it takes shelter behind lies. Even if he has broken the window-pane and is blatantly denying the act, severe punishment is not the solution to the problem. The child cannot be reformed through beating and punishment alone. Nor can there be any guarantee that the child will not commit similar acts again. The parents in such circumstances must bear in their minds that the child by nature is not aggressive. There is always an external reason for such behavior.

Therefore, they must investigate the matter carefully to determine the actual reasons and cause for the act of destruction. When the cause for the breaking of the glass is determined, then there will not be motivation for the child perpetrating such an act again. Perhaps, the act of vandalism was a direct result of some insult caused to the child by some one. Perhaps, the child had not been receiving proper attention and he took out his spleen by causing damage to the window. It could be the reaction to some undeserved punishment the child had received from his parents.

If the parents make efforts to remove the psychological complexes from the mind of the child, there is every possibility of setting him right. If such a breakthrough is achieved, there will not be any need for punitive action. The child will then refrain from destructive acts and there will nod be need to shout at him or beat him.

1. If you learn that your child has done something wrong, and you desire to guide him to the right path, then don't interrogate him like a policeman. It is possible that to protect his ego the child might have recourse to lies. It is better in such circumstances not

to interrogate him and say as, for instance, that he must return the book that he had borrowed from his friend. Tell him that it is not proper to keep other's things for long. Return your friend's book immediately with an apology.

2. Don't threaten the child with a punishment that you are not intending to give. For example, don't tell him that if he did such and such a thing, you would beat him, or you would hand him over to the police, or that you will send him out of the house. Also don't tell him in your anger that you would not take him to the forthcoming dinner he had been eagerly looking forward to. With such false threats you would be teaching the child to tell lies. You must convey to the child only such things that you really intend doing, and you think that they are right by him.

3. The parents who are strict with their children and expect from them much more than their capability, are perhaps pushing them more towards lying. For example, if the child is not good at studies and unmindful of this the parents insist on his coming rst in the class, keep nagging him every day about his lessons and shout at him.

Because the child has limited capability and with his best efforts he is unable to rise to the occasion. Since the child wants the goodwill of the parents, he may take shelter behind lies. Or he will make an excuse that at the time of the examination he suffered from a headache. Sometimes he would say that the teacher doesn't like him and has given him a poorer grade.

If the parents had properly assessed the capacity of the child, they wouldn't have put him in the position of making false excuses.

1. There are parents who attribute any wrong act of their child to his companions at school or at play. Sometimes they even blame

animals and plants for such things. For example: they might say that a cat or a rat has been responsible for that These ignorant parents think that they are doing something good by their child not attributing an act to him that he has really committed. But there are two very pronounced disadvantages of this: rstly, they are encouraging the child to tell lies and secondly, the child will learn to shift the blame for his own acts on others.

2. If sometimes your children tell lies unintentionally, then explore the reasons thereof and search for a remedy. But this exploration should be done in a subtle way that the children don't start feeling that an investigation is on against them.

Keeping Promises

The human society cannot function without the institution of promises and assurances of their fulllment. People make agreements and covenants with one another that goes to make families and clans. There will be agreements between cities that meld them together.

People give great importance to these covenants because they are the basis of their collective lives. Keeping promises is an important aspect of human life and every person considers it very bad to do anything in infringement of a promise. Every person who enters into a covenant with another expects that the terms of the contract will be adhered to implicitly.

Whichever groups abide by the terms of their covenant will be termed as well organized units. The reason for their well being is that they will have trust on one another without any reason for conict. The lives of their people will be successful and contented. To the contrary the people of an area that doesn't abide by its covenants with others will suffer from a feeling of uncertainty and unrest. They will be victims of perpetual conflict.

Every individual or society who respect the agreements made with others will have the respect and confidence of others. Those who break their covenants will be abhorred and looked down upon by the others. Islam is a religion of nature that lays great stress on fulllment of promises.

Allah says in the Holy The Holy Qur'an:

> "…. and fulll (every) engagement, for (every) engagement will be enquired into (on the Day of Reckoning). " (The Holy Qur'an, 17:34)

At another place in the The Holy Qur'an it is said:

> "Those who faithfully observe their trusts and their covenants," (The Holy Qur'an, 23:8)

The Prophet of Islam said:

"The person who has no covenant has no faith."[144]

"Whoever has faith in Allah and the Day of Reckoning, should fulll his promises."[145] 'Ali has said to Malik al Ashtar:

"Breaking promises makes others unhappy as also Allah will be unhappy."[146]

"Where you cannot keep your promise, don't make one. Where you cannot discharge a guarantee, don't give one."[147]

To perpetuate the habit of keeping promises and abiding by

---

[144] Bihar al-anwar, v75, p. 96

[145] Usul al-Ka, v 2, p. 364

[146] Bihar al-anwar, v77, p. 96

[147] Gharar al-hukm, p. 801

covenants in the society, it is imperative to train the people from their very childhood to be true to their word. This training starts with the childhood in the environment of the family. The child emulates the actions and words of the parents. The parents can set an example for the children.

By nature, the child expects that promises will be kept. When the parents fulll their small promises the child gets trained in this important aspect of life. But if they take their small promises lightly and neglect them, the child takes the negative example and develops the habit of breaking his word. They start believing that promises are made to be broken.

If the parents make false promises to momentarily calm the child, they are inadvertently training the child to make false promises Can such children grow into respectable individuals? To quieten the child the mother promises to buy him sweets, ice cream., toys etc Sometimes she makes these promises to make him take the bitter medicine or to get him vaccinated.

She frightens him by saying that if he did a certain thing, she would send him to the police, report him to his Dad or deny him new dress for the festival. If you consider the lives of the people around you, or your own life, there will be innumerable instances of such false promises and threats made to the innocent children. Do the parents ever imagine what impact they are making on the impressionable minds of the children? This injustice is perpetrated on the innocent children quite innocuously!

The ignorant parents don't know that they are sinning by making false promises and also they are training the child to follow in their footsteps.

This is the reason Islam requires the parents to keep the promises that they make with their children.

The Prophet of Islam has said:

"Love the children. Treat them with kindness and if you make a promise to them, fulll it without fail. The children think that you are the provider of sustenance for them."[148]

'Ali, The Commander of the Faithful, says:

"Whenever you make a promise to the children, denitely keep it."[149]

---

[148] Wasail al-shiah, v 15, p. 101, Bihar al-anwar, v104, p. 92

[149] Mustadrak al-wasail, v 2, p. 106

Ownership

Love for the mother is a part of human nature. Man wants to own the things that he needs. He thinks he is the master of these things. He also expects others to respect his sentiment about his belongings. This instinct of ownership in the human nature cannot be completely obliterated. Whichever way it is curbed, it will rise again.

Ownership, although a notional phenomenon, is such a phenomenon that has assumed the garb of reality. Without the sense of ownership the running of human life seems impossible. From the time a child starts recognizing himself, he identies his needs, he instinctively thinks that he owns them.

When a child gets a thing lying on the oor, or takes it from someone else's hands, he thinks that it belongs to him. He will not readily part with it. He knows that he is the owner of his clothes, shoes, toys and other things. He doesn't like others handling these things.

You must have noticed that children love their toys, however bad shape might they be in. They protect them and even ght for them. They have pride of ownership in their natures. If someone rises to protect his rights, he should not be counted as evil. Sense of ownership is not a negative instinct. The parents must accept the child's natural instinct.

It often happens that the children trespass over the ownership of other children and try to usurp the toys of other children. The parents should prevent such acts. If an older child bullies the smaller ones, the parents must intervene in a just manner. They must be convinced that they should not take away the toys of younger siblings by force. If the attitude continues even after this, the child must be strictly warned to behave. The human needs are ever growing. If some control is not asserted on them, the needs might surpass the means. They can also become the cause of destruction of the person.

The concept of ownership is for fullling the legitimate needs of persons. Work is deemed essential for achieving ownership. Love for wealth in legitimate limits is considered good. But if it exceeds certain limits, it can come under the category of avarice and parsimony. There are lots of people who can be termed mammon worshippers. They keep running after wealth tirelessly. They even compromise their rest, self-respect and honor in this futile search for wealth. It is a type of madness. They only want to create hordes of wealth that are useful neither to them nor to others. .These persons cannot be termed wise.

Therefore, the parents should encourage the sense of ownership in the child and also teach him to be contented with what he can acquire legitimately. He should have toys, but not too many of them. The toys should be sufcient to play and learn and not too many to create a hoard. If the child has too many new toys that are lying in the shelf, the parents should better give some to other children.

But this should be done discreetly by telling the child that he has many toys and the other child has none. If he gave him some, he will be happy. You will also be pleasing your parents and Allah too. The child will then be happy in parting with some of his toys. The child wants to please his parents. This instinct encourages him to listen to them and part with some of his possessions.

This way the habit of sharing things is cultivated in the child. Sometimes the parents can encourage the child to lend his toys to other children for playing and return. This way the spirit of co-operation and sharing can be cultivated in the child.

In a nutshell the parents should keep in mind that there is moderation in all aspects of upbringing of the child. They should promote the sense of ownership in the child and see that it does not exceed certain limits. They must ensure that the child does not become a blind lover of wealth in his future life.

Magnanimity

Generosity and magnanimity are excellent traits in a person. A magnanimous person strives hard to acquire wealth, but he will not have excessive attachment to riches. He wants wealth, but to share it with others. He doesn't believe in hoarding wealth. He spends his life with his family and wholeheartedly participates in the welfare activities of the community. He helps the deprived and the needy. He makes the right use of his wealth.

A parsimonious person hoards wealth. He neither spends it on himself nor gives a helping hand to the needy. Such a person will be amassing wealth for the posterity.

Islam has condemned miserliness and praised generosity in very clear terms. The Prophet of Islam says:

"Generosity is a part of *iman* (the Faith) and the *iman* shall take one to the Heaven."[150]

"Generosity is such a tree in the Heaven the branches of which have reached the Earth. Whosoever caught hold of one of the branches,

---

[150] Jam'i al Sa'adat, v 2, p. 113

he will reach the Heaven."[151] *"Behisht* (the Heaven) is the home of the generous people."[152] "Allah is Municent and Generous and likes generosity in men."[153] The Prophet of Islam said:

"It is not proper for the mumin (the pious) to be miserly and cowardly."[154]

Generosity and magnanimity attract hearts and affections. People like a generous person and respect him. With generosity and magnanimity hearts can be subdued.

The Prophet of Islam says:

"A generous person is closer to Allah's creations and the Heaven. He is away from the Hell. The miserly person is away from Allah, His creations (the men) and the Heaven. But he is closer to the Hell Fire."[155]

A miserly person doesn't pay the legitimate rights. He therefore becomes eligible of the Retribution on the Day of Reckoning. .Generosity makes a person acceptable here and also in the Hereafter. The quality of generosity is instinctive as are the other virtues of men. But the parents have to nourish these qualities in their children.

It is true that every child is born with his own individual nature, but some natures readily accept to become generous and others tend towards miserliness. The parents training and upbringing can have important effect on the moulding of the natures of the children. They can inuence the child in curbing the miserly tendencies to a greater extent and encourage him to be more generous.

The thing that has the maximum effect on the child's progress is

---

[151] Jam'i al Sa'adat, v 2, p. 114

[152] Jam'i al Sa'adat, v 2, p. 114

[153] Jam'i al Sa'adat, v 4, p. 113

[154] Jam'i al Sa'adat, v 2, p. 112

[155] al-mahajjatul bayda,v 3, p. 248

the character of the parents. The parents are always the role models for the children. If the parents are generous in spending on good causes, the children too will try to emulate them. In stages this habit of generosity takes root in the nature of the children. If, to the contrary, the parents are miserly, the children too will mould themselves on the same pattern. Habits go a long way in moulding characters.

'Ali, The Commander of the Faithful, says:

"Train yourself to be generous, select the best of virtues and these virtues will become your habit."[156]

"Generosity is amongst good habits."[157]

Imam Ja'far as-Sadiq said:

"To be a sinner it is sufcient for a person to spend nothing for his family and deprive them."[158]

Parents can make use of the following guidelines for cultivating the habits of generosity and magnanimity in their children:

1. Encourage the child to give a part of the things he has to the parents and his other siblings. The child must be suitably praised for the generous act and thanked. .In the beginning the child may be reluctant to part with his possession, but, by and by, he will get into the habit of being generous. When the child is reluctant for this experiment, he should not be forced into giving. This might make the child stubborn.
2. Sometimes encourage the child to allow other children to play with his toys. The child should also be encouraged to share his sweets and chocolates with other children. When he does it, give him a pat on his back.

---

[156] Bihar al-anwar, v 77, p. 213

[157] Gharar al hukm, p. 17

[158] Wasail al-shiah, v 15, p. 251

3. Sometimes encourage him to give a part of his pocket money to the poor and the needy. Or ask him to spend some money for any good cause. If this becomes a habit, it would have a salutary effect on the character of the child as he grows up.
4. Ask the child to invite his friends home for a meal and see that he entertains them with care.
5. The parents can give some money to the child everyday to be given as alms or for some good cause.
6. Discuss with the child the difculties and hardships of poor people. If possible take him along with you to the hospital, the orphanage and the home for the poor and aged. In his presence help some needy persons

This way the child can be initiated into the habit of generosity. We, however, cannot claim that this method will work on all the children. The parents should make their best efforts and the success can differ from child to child. Every individual has his own nature and the capacity to accept change. For the children their habits also come as a genetic factor inherited from generation to generation. But careful breeding can denitely have some good effect.

A lady writes in a letter thus:

"…. At a pleasant place we had an orchard. Different varieties of fruits used to grow there in abundance. My Mom and Granny used to send some fruits to the needy. They were particularly generous to such of those needy persons who were serving our family. They used to entrust this task to me. From the age of six or seven years I got into the habit of doing this work. In the village there were families of two blind persons.

My heart used to feel much for them. Every day when I visited them, I used to catch their hands, bring them out for some fresh air and take them back to their homes. .I used to bring fresh water for them from the lake. These blind men used to bless me and pray for me. When I told my Mom and Dad about this, they were very pleased. My mom said, one who has become blind is really deserving of all help.

My parents always used to encourage me for doing good deeds. I used to save from my pocket money and give to the needy. Slowly I got habituated of doing this. I am now a member of a social help organisation that is taking care of fourteen needy families.

My children too have taken good effect from my attitude. One day a child said,' Give me some money every morning.' I asked him, ' Why?' he said, ' I shall save this money' I give him the money regularly and remind him not to waste it. After some days he came to me with his treasure-trove. He had forty- eight coins in that. He said, ' Mom, if you permit me, I shall give the money to a blind person. He lives on the way to our school.' I was very pleased with the child and I kissed and hugged him."

1. Jam'i al Sa'adat, v 2, p. 113

A Helping Hand in Good Work

Certain tasks that are big and important cannot be accomplished single-handed. But if there is some help available, the same job is done with ease. If man keeps working alone he will fall behind in doing many tasks. It seldom happens that a single person starts and runs an organisations for social welfare. An individual cannot run a hospital, school, mosque, orphanage, library etc without having others to help him. In fact, a person cannot even manage the administration of any such organization individually. But with others' help and co-operation the work can be accomplished to perfection. Any nation where the population has the spirit of mutual help and co-operation will be a prosperous nation.

In this respect Islam is a complete congregational system that invites people to come together for common good. The Holy The Holy Qur'an says:

> *"Help ye (one another) in righteousness and piety, and help ye not (one another) in sin and aggression."* (The Holy

Qur'an, 5:4)

'Ali, The Commander of the Faithful, says:
"Co-operating to withhold the truth is delity and probity."[159]

The spirit of co-operation and camaraderie takes root from childhood only. Luckily human beings have gregarious nature by birth. But there is always the need to utilize this instinct to advantage. The parents who are keen to give good upbringing to their children encourage the instinct of fellowship in them and provide to them toys and games that need group participation.

They can give them toys that need assembling by more than one child. They can encourage them to have a jointly save their money for use for a good cause with guidance from the parents. With this collective saving they can buy fruits and sweets to distribute to the sickly, poor and needy.

The parents can add some money to this amount and also help them to buy and distribute the fruits etc. They can also give the savings periodically to some welfare organization. They may also give the money to some public library to help buy new books. The parents can also encourage the children to form a small committee and initiate some welfare activity by themselves.

If the parents are members of a welfare organization, they should initiate the children too to the activity. They can give some money to the child to personally contribute to the fund of the organization and make him a regular member.

---

[159] Gharar al hukm, p. 48

Humaneness and Children

All are Gods creations. All humans are the off springs of the same rst parents.(Adam and Eve. In fact all men belong to the same large family. Allah has created them and He likes them. He has assured sustenance to everyone. Allah only has endowed them with all their necessities in the world. He has given them control over the manipulation and use of these things. He has given them wisdom and strength to gainfully utilize the things around them to their advantage.

Allah has provided them the opportunities to raise their spirits to reach perfection in piety and earn rewards in the Hereafter. He provided the means of guidance in the forms of Prophets from time to time. He has Ordained (*mansus*) .the Imams and then there are the religious guides, the *mujtahids* and *maraja'h*.

All this because Allah loves men and He is extremely Municent. He wants men to be kind to one another and strive for the general welfare. He wants men to assist each other both in fair weather and during calamitous conditions. Those who have welfare of other human beings in their thoughts and actions are the chosen people of Allah. They shall have plenty of rewards in the Hereafter. Islam, a gregarious Faith, has given particular emphasis to the need for service to humanity.

The Prophet of Islam has said:

"All men eat the food provided by Allah. Therefore from men the dearest to Allah are those who give sustenance to other men and please some families."[160]

Imam Ja'far as-Sadiq says:

"Allah says that people eat the food given by Me. Such of those men are dear to me who are kind to the other humans and strive hard to help them in the time of need."[161]

Someone asked the Prophet:

"Who is the dearest to Allah among men?' The Prophet replied:

'One who is most benecial to other fellow-men."[162] The Prophet of Islam has said:

"After the Faith, the wisest act for a person is the love and care of the other human beings, be they good or otherwise."[163]

"One who is not concerned with the good of the Muslims is not a Muslim."[164] Imam Ja'far as-Sadiq says:

"Allah's preferred men are those who are approached by men in need of help. These preferred men of Allah will be in the Care of Allah on the Day of Judgment."[165]

The Prophet of Islam said:

"Allah is Kind on His men and likes those men who are kind to their

---

[160] Bihar al-anwar, v74, p. 317

[161] Bihar al-anwar, v 73, p. 337

[162] Bihar al-anwar, v74, p. 239

[163] Bihar al-anwar, v74, p. 392

[164] Bihar al-anwar, v74, p. 347

[165] Bihar al-anwar, v 74, p. 318

fellow men."[166]

There are hundreds of such traditions of the Prophet and the Imams that are spread over many compendiums of the sayings of these Infallible Persons.

The Prophet has seen the Islamic society as a single unit and has asked the followers of the Faith to work for the common good. Islam is a Gregarious Faith and considers the welfare of individuals as the welfare of the society. It ghts against all kinds of selshness. A true Muslim can never be selsh and will never overlook the rights of others in the society.

Friendship for other human beings is a superior quality and it is imbued in the nature of every individual. But with proper training this quality can be made manifest. Sometimes it may happen that this wonderful quality might totally disappear from the nature of some individuals.

This is like other inherent instincts in all human being which start manifesting during early childhood in their rudiments and if they are not properly nourished, they might become dormant or totally recede into the recesses of the individual's mind. It is the responsibility of the parents to make their children friendly to human beings and generous. If the parents themselves are generous to others and the children see the shades of generosity in their words and actions, they can naturally follow suit.

The responsible and informed parents sometimes describe the plight of the needy people, the poor, the handicapped and old, in the presence of their children. If possible they take out the children to meet these people. They tell the children that these are the deprived people and are in need of support and help. They provide help to such people in the presence of the children to set a good example for them to emulate

---

[166] Bihar al-anwar, v 74, p. 339

when they grow up and are capable of helping others.

The parents sometimes describe to the children the unfair tyranny heaped by some people on hapless persons and also the pathetic condition of the unfortunate sufferers. They also talk to their children about the unfortunate orphans who don't have parents to look after them and they deserve full support from others in the society. They take their children to the orphanage to meet these kids and sometimes invite some of them to their home. All this goes a long way in making the children realize their responsibility to help and assist the needy in the society.

Justice and Equality

A family consisting of a few members is like a small society and the parents manage the affairs of this small habitation. As running a country is not possible without justice and equality, so is the management of a household not possible without these concomitant factors; namely Justice and equality for all.

Selessness, love, affection and unity is possible only in an environment of justice and equality. The children will get proper upbringing in this atmosphere. The inherent traits of the children will nd expression and they will learn to be just and fair from the example set to them by their parents. If the parents are ignorant of the need for justice and fair play, so will be their children.

Imam Ja'far as-Sadiq says:

"As pure and cool water is craved for by a thirsty person, so do people desire to have justice and equality and their taste is sweeter and better for them. There is nothing better than justice."[167]

"Three types of persons will be closer to Allah on the Day of

---

[167] Usul al-Ka, v 2, p. 147

Reckoning: First: Those who are not cruel to their subordinates in times of anger. Second: Those who go to mediate between two litigants, but don't do anything against the requirement of justice. Third: Those who always uphold the truth, even if they come to personal harm by doing so."[168]

Allah says in the Holy The Holy Qur'an:

"Allah orders for Justice and Fairness." *(The Holy Qur'an, 16:90)*

Just and equitable parents treat all their children equally. They don't show particular preference for any particular child. Be it a son or a daughter, pretty or not so pretty, capable or mediocre; the parents have the same feelings of love and affection for all of them. They give equitable treatment to all their children

The Prophet of Islam has said:

"Keep justice for all your children in your mind even when some of them are away. If you desire treatment of love, kindness and justice from your children, then give them similar treatment."[169]

The Prophet noticed that a person was more attached to one son than to the other. He told him: "Who don't you keep the need for justice and equality of treatment in mind?"[170]

One person was sitting in the company of the Prophet when his son arrived. The person kissed the boy and made him sit on his lap. After a while the person's daughter came there and the person made her sit in front of him. Then the Prophet told to the person: "Why didn't you keep in your consideration the need for justice and equality between

---

[168] Bihar al-anwar, v 75, p. 33

[169] Makarim al akhlaq, v 71, p. 252

[170] Makarim al akhlaq, v 11, p. 252

your children?"[171]

'Ali, The Commander of the Faithful, says:
"Delivering justice and equality to people is the best of politics."[172]

One woman came to the presence of the Prophet's wife, Ayesha, with her two little children. Ayesha gave her three dates. The mother gave one each to the two children and then equally divided the third date and gave one to each of them. When the Prophet returned home, Ayesha narrated the incident to him.

The Prophet said:
"Why are you surprised at the action of that woman? For keeping justice and equality in view Allah will give her a place in the Heaven!!"[173]

If the parents treat their children unjustly in a partial manner they will create a very harmful impression on them.

1. The children will take after the unjust attitude of the parents and behave the same way with others. With time this attitude will become a part of their natures.
2. The children who had been the victims of injustice from their parents will carry rancor for them in their minds It is possible they turn rebellious and disobedient.
3. With treatment of injustice and partiality there is chance of jealousy and enmity springing up between brothers and sisters and it might go to the limit of sometimes harming each other.
4. The children who have received unjust treatment at the hands of their parents will have feelings of dejection and oppression that will get engraved in their minds. It is quite possible that later on they develop psychic disorders.

---

[171] Majma al zawaid, v 8, p. 156

[172] Gharar al hukm, p. 64

[173] Sunan, Ibn Majah,v72, p. 1210

The parents will be responsible for all the consequences of their partial and unjust treatment meted out to their children.

But the parents, in all fairness, give equitable treatment to all their children. At different ages the children will have differing requirements. Because they are born at different times and are of different sexes, they may not have similar requirements all the time. The law of justice and equality too is not rigid about equal treatment in such differing circumstances. Will it be right to lift the elder child in your lap like you do to a babe in the cradle?

Similarly, will it be right to give the same amount of pocket money to a child of three years as is given to his sibling who is eighteen years old. Can a daughter be given the same freedom of movement that is given to a grown up son? Fair play and justice don't approve of any such concessions and we too don't recommend them.

The parents must thoughtfully adopt such fair and just standards of treatment for their children that they don't give rise to the feelings of partiality in some of them. This matter has been dealt at some length in the chapter on Jealousy which you may refer.

One person writes in his memoirs:

"The memory of my childhood is very bitter and I am unable to forget it. Dad used to discriminate between us brothers. He used to comply with all his wishes and never for once considered my wants. He used to treat my brother with respect and treated me insultingly. Father loved him more and always had kind words for him.

As a result of this treatment I started thinking that Dad and my brother are not good. I used to think of taking revenge on my Dad for the unjust behavior with me. In my worried state I preferred to be alone by myself. I started spitting on the walls and tarnishing them. I used to break the glass window-panes to take out my spleen. What was the alternative for me? But Dad was totally unconcerned about this. He didn't know that my actions were solely to harm his interest."

One lady writes in her diary:

"…. One of our closest relatives had two daughters One was a good student and very bright while the other was mediocre. Both used to go to the school. The elder daughter, who was not bright, used to secure lower grades in her examinations. The younger girl always used to perform very well in her studies. Their mother always used to brag about the brilliance of her younger daughter and run down the elder one. She used to be full of praise for the younger daughter and always criticized the elder one that she was wasting all the expense incurred on her schooling. She even used to say that all the good dresses and food given to her is a waste.

The same elder daughter is now married. She has several children. She is an ordinary housewife. She gives an unhealthy look and seems a victim of inferiority complex. She looks tired and lost in her thoughts. At parties she takes a quiet corner and doesn't converse with others.

When I egg her on to talk, she only takes a sigh and says,' about what can I talk?' I remember, prior to her marriage, I took her to a psychiatrist. The doctor, after a long session of discussion with her, said that there was nothing wrong with her. In fact, her parents are sick that they have not treated her properly and reduced her to the present plight.

Once the doctor asked her, 'Can you cook?' She started crying and said,' I can cook. But whenever I prepare anything my parents say that my younger sister cooks better food.'"

Respect for the Children

The child too is a human being and every human being instinctively loves oneself. He wishes that others recognize his worth and respect him. When others show respect to him he feels proud and thinks that he has been praised. The parents who love their children should show them due consideration and respect. In the training of a child, showing respect to him is considered as a very important element.

The child who receives respect and estimation will grow into a sober and respectable person. He always tries to maintain his reputation and refrains from doing anything wrong. He tries to keep doing good things to rise in the estimation of others. The child who is not treated by his parents with due respect, he tries to emulate them while dealing with others. The child is a man in miniature and like all men he loves himself. He will be displeased if he is not treated properly and with respect.

The parents who treat children badly without giving any thought to their hurt feelings, create rancor in their young minds. Sooner or later such children turn hostile and become stubbornly difcult. Ignorant parents, whose number unfortunately is not small, consider that treating the children with respect spoils them. They take cool, condescending, and vain attitude towards the children. This way they crush the personality of the children and give birth to the inferiority complex in their impressionable minds.

From the point of view of good breeding this attitude of the parents proves a major impediment. If the parents treat their children with respect, then the child will try to reciprocate. The child will get the understanding from that very tender age that the parents treat him humanely and give him importance. He will therefore abstain from doing anything that is not considered good in the society.

He will try to do good things to maintain the respectable treatment he has been receiving from the parents. It is a matter of concern that in our societies the children are not treated with respect. They are not treated as members of the family till they are grown up. In parties and celebrations they are generally not invited and go with the parents as appendages.

In parties they are seated at an insignicant corner When they arrive at the party and leave it, they are not given any attention. In the car they will not have any space for themselves. They either go standing or sit on the lap of the father. They are not allowed to speak in the party. And even if they take courage in their hands to speak, they don't get any attention from the elders. They are summoned, if ever, with indecorum.

Islam gives all attention to the need for showing respect to the children. The Prophet of Islam has said: "Respect your children and give them good training so that Allah rewards you."

'Ali, The Commander of the Faithful, says:

"The meanest person is one who shows disrespect to others."[174]

The Prophet always, and everywhere, used to treat children with

---

[174] Bihar al-anwar, v 104, p. 45

affection and respect. Whenever he returned from his travels, the children used to run out and receive him. He used to hug and kiss them. Some of the children used to mount with him on the steed. He used to ask his other companions to take the other children on their horses. This way he used to enter the ramparts of the city.

Insulting behaviour with children, even with babes in arms, is forbidden. Umm al Fadhl says:

"The Prophet, when Imam Husayn was a babe in the arms, one day took him from me and hugged him, the child wet his clothes. I snatched Husayn away from the Prophet at that moment, when the child started crying. The Prophet told me, 'Umm al Fazl, Keep your cool. Water can clean my clothes. But who will remove the displeasure and hurt of the child Husayn.'"[175]

One gentleman writes:

"I had no signicance in the consideration of my parents. Not only that they did not have any respect for me, they used to insult and admonish me time and again. They never allowed me to do any work. If ever I took initiative to do some work, they used to nd fault. They used to insult me in the presence of their friends and mine.

They never allowed me to say anything while others were around. All these things made me carry the feelings of inferiority and shame for myself. I started considering myself a useless person. Now that I am a grown up man, I continue to labour under the same feelings of dejection. If I am confronted with difcult tasks, I feel myself helpless and incapable of doing it.

I feel that because I am unable to have my own opinion about my capability, others should volunteer their opinion about me. I consider myself insignicant and absolutely incapable. I have no condence on myself. Even I nd myself at a loss to speak in the presence of others.

---

[175] Hadiya al ahbab, p. 176

When I utter something in such situations, I ponder for hours whether what I said was right for the occasion or not."

Self-Assessment and Meaningful Existence

The entire lives of the animals are spent in eating, sleeping, and breeding. The intelligence and knowledge of animals is imperfect. They are unable to discriminate between good and bad. Therefore they don't have any responsibility imposed on them. They will not be required to account for their deeds.

There is no preordained responsibility for them. But man, who is the best of the creations of Allah, is not like the animals. Man has wisdom and capability. He can discriminate between good and bad, pretty and ugly. Man has been created for a perpetual and eternal existence and not for extinction.

Therefore he carries a great responsibility and duty ordained for him. Man is the vicegerent and trustee of Allah in this world. The purpose of the life of the man is not just eating, sleeping, satisfying desires and procreation. But the man has to tread such a path that he proves himself even more superior than the angels. He is human and must strive to promote his humanity. Man should have a goal in life. The goal has to be idealistic. Man strives in Allah's cause and to serve His creations and not only for achieving the worldly benets. Man has to search the Truth and to follow the Truth.

Yes the human existence is such a precious jewel which is far superior than all the animals. It is a shame that lot of men have squandered their invaluable worth. They spend their lives literally like animals. In their view eating, drinking, sleeping, fullling carnal desires alone are the purpose of their lives. It is possible that a person might live for a hundred years without understanding himself and die in utter ignorance, He comes into the world like an animal and will die an animal He will remain aimless and itinerant all his life. The result of all his striving will be nought.

Man should know himself. Who is he? From where he has come? Where he has to go? What is the purpose of his birth? What path he must take? What is the real goal and what is auspicious for him?

'Ali, The Commander of the Faithful, says:

"The best enlightenment is that the man recognizes himself, and the greatest ignorance is when a person doesn't know his own self."[176]

"One who did not recognize himself, he strayed from the path of salvation, and took the road to ignorance and aimlessness."[177]

"For Allah the most abhorrent person is one who has made eating and satisfaction of carnal desires the sole purpose of life."[178]

"One who has made achievement of Salvation on the Day of Judgment his purpose in life will get fullment."[179]

The parents should give the lesson of self-assessment and purposeful existence to their children. They can progressively give a purposeful character to the lives of the children. The child, with the help of the parents, should be helped to know himself. From where he has come?

---

[176] Gharar al hukm, p. 179

[177] Gharar al hukm, p. 77

[178] Gharar al hukm, p. 205

[179] Gharar al hukm, p. 693

What is the purpose of his existence? Where he will go ultimately? What are his duties and responsibilities in this world? With what program and aim he should live his life? If the parents know themselves and have denite aims in life, then they will be successfully able to guide their children on the desired path.

The Income of the Household and Expenses

In the management of a house, the most vital aspect is the control of the purse strings. Any sensible household would keep track of their regular income and expenditure. As it is said, they cut the coat according to the length of the cloth available. They make efforts to keep their expenses within the amount of inow of cash into the family's account.

Every family should know their priorities and allocate money to different items of expense on that basis. Careful families always try that they don't fall into debt trap. They will thus avoid unnecessary worries coming their way. Even if their economic condition is bad for a time, they plan and overcome these difculties in some time. They avoid reducing themselves to the status of penury through proper management of their limited resources.

Contrary to this the families that are careless about proper management of their expenses, who are extravagant and continue living beyond their means, fall into the habit of compulsive borrowing. To meet the bills for their expenses, they are forced even to borrow money at high rates of interest. Since they are compulsive borrowers, they don't mind buying expensive things on credit.

Such families are never free of worries. They come to such a pass that sometimes they are not able to buy the basic necessities of day to day living. Such things happen even to families whose incomes are reasonably sound. They will be in their straitened circumstances because of not having a proper plan for expenditure. These people are the victims of false pomp and show. The welfare of the family depends not only on earning and bringing some money home, but it also requires proper budgeting and control of the expenses.

Imam Ja'far as-Sadiq says:

"When Allah wants a family to prosper, then he gives them the capability of wisdom and order in life."[180]

"All excellence is assembled in three things: One of them is making use of understanding and prudence in managing their nances."[181]

"Extravagance becomes the cause of poverty and penury, and moderation in life provides contentment and comfort."[182]

'Ali, The Commander of the Faithful, says:

"With thrift, half the requirements can be met."[183]

"There are three signs of an extravagant person: 1. He wants to eat what he has not. 2. He buys the thing for which he has no money. 3. He wears the dress which he doesn't afford to buy."[184]

To streamline the nancial affairs of the family it is essential that the husband and wife should have similarity of views. If the husband or the wife spends without keeping in mind the priorities, then the management of the house will go haywire.

---

[180] Usul al-Ka, v 5, p. 88

[181] Usul al-Ka, v 5, p. 87

[182] Wasail al-shiah, v 12, p. 41

[183] Mustadrak al-wasail, v 2, p. 424

[184] Wasail al-shiah, v 21, p. 41

Secondly, even the children should have some understanding of the needs and priorities. If the children become thoughtlessly extravagant and the parents, out of their love, humor them and permit their spending sprees, the family can come into nancial problems at some stage.

The parents should inform the children the nancial status of the family and discuss the budget in their presence. This will give them an understanding of the importance of thrift in spending. They should also know that the management of a house is not all bed of roses.

It is essential that the children should, in stages, be made acquainted with the household chores and also the income of the family. They should know that the house runs on the income of the parents and they have no other means besides that. They should understand that all the needs of the house have to be met from that money only.

They should also be told that expenditure on certain matters have to be given priority over others. For example the household expenses, the house-rent , the bill for amenities like power/water etc. In the rst instance the expenses on necessities have to be met. Then the other requirements can follow. The children need to understand and extend their co-operation to the parents in this matter.

From the very childhood the children should be trained to match their needs and demands to the means of the family. They must be stopped from wasteful expense and thoughtless purchasing. They must be introduced to the habit of thrift and they should consider themselves as members of the family who have to spend within the means of the family. They should not get a false notion that they are from a rich

family and they can spend as they wish. They must be trained to control their wishes in the interest of the essential expenses of the family that cannot be avoided or postponed.

These children, when they grow up, will have the reins of the society in their hands. Therefore they must be groomed into the habit of thrift from the very childhood. However comfortable the nancial status of the parents the children must be taught to spend money carefully and judiciously. They should explain to the children that all men belong to one family of human beings.

Therefore the fortunate ones who are rich should give help to the poor. If the income of the family is insufcient, they must prune their daily expenses and try to make the ends meet within their meager resources. The parents should not complain to their children about the nancial straits they are in. They should instead of this give the lesson of patience and trust on Allah.

Prepare them to face the odds in their future life with courage and equanimity. When a child is capable of working, initiate him into work and give him the moral support. They must tell to the child that if he starts working, his wages will supplement the family's income and they will thus be more comfortable.

The child must be encouraged to give a portion of his earnings for the household expenses. This way he will appreciate his responsibility for the family. A young earning member of the family should draw his pocket money from his wages keeping in mind the requirements of the household expenses.

Respect for the Law

People in a civilized society cannot live without law. Where the law of the jungle prevails, that is not a civilized society. To run the administration of a society very well dened laws are absolutely essential. These laws are for upholding order and providing protection to the aggrieved and dispensing punishment to the guilty.

For the comfort and safety of the populace, laws are absolutely necessary. In the countries where there is good understanding between the people and the lawmakers, the laws are made for the benet of the people and they therefore respect the laws. There can be general well being if the people in a country are law abiding.

In countries where the lawmakers work with ulterior selsh motives, and while framing the statute they don't have the welfare of the people in mind, the people stop honoring the law and there can be unrest in such societies. Unfortunately, earlier our country faced a similar situation (Here the author means Iran of the Shah's period).

Most of the laws were neither Islamic nor good for the people. The laws were formulated keeping in mind the ruling clique and the wishes of the Imperialists and their stooges. No attention was given to the plight of the worker, the toiler and the deprived populace.

The lawmakers tried to hoodwink the people with oppressive and repressive laws to subjugate the masses.

But since the people of Iran felt that those un-Islamic statutes were against their interests, they had no respect for them. However there were some laws in that statute that were good for the people. But since the legal system was anti-people in totality, they rejected the complete system.

Respect for legitimate and people-friendly laws is essential and the parents have to explain about them to the children. When a child nds the parents crossing the road from the zebra crossing only, he feels that he must do likewise. He gets into the habit of following this rule of safety and may never transgress it.

The parents must tell the children that the cars and other fast moving vehicles have the right of way on the roads and the pedestrians can only use the zebra crossings when they require to cross to the other side of the road. Pedestrians trespassing on the roads commit an offence and also are exposed to the risk of accidents. When the child understands the advantage of abiding by the law, he becomes a good citizen.

'Ali, The Commander of the Faithful, says:

"Habits are second nature !"[185]

---

[185] Gharar al hukm, p. 26

Respect

It is always the wish of the parents that their children are well behaved. Good and polite children are a source of pride for every parent. The well behaved children politely greet the person they visit, shake hands with him, enquire about his health, converse softly, limit the conversation to what is asked of them and say proper adieus when departing from the hosts place. Such children give due respect to the elders, when elders arrive they politely stand up, show deference to the scholars, religious gures and generally respect pious and good persons.

In a gathering they remain cool and collected, don't talk loudly, thank the person who gives them something, don't interrupt others, particularly the elders during conversations. They say Bismillah (In the name of Allah the Benecent the Merciful), the Islamic Grace, before starting to eat, they take small morsels of food, don't eat excessively, don't throw food on the table or the oor and follow all the required table manners.

They take care of their dresses that they don't get stained and try to remain clean and tidy. They will be considerate to the others and never hurt others feelings. They walk with a decent gait and give the impression of being obedient and decent children. They don't ridicule others with practical jokes and when someone speaks to them, they listen with rapt attention.

It is not only the parents who like polite children, but they are popular with all who happen to interact with them. Impertinent and impolite children are abhorred by all.

The Commander of the Faithful, 'Ali, says:

"Respectability is the zenith of humanity."[186]

"Respect (politeness) in a man is like pretty raiment."[187]

"Good behavior (politeness) is required by people more than silver or gold."[188] "There is no better embellishment than politeness in a man."[189]

"The best inheritance a father can give to his son is to train him to be of polite."[190] "An impolite person will have more failings."[191]

Imam Ja'far as-Sadiq says:

"Allow your child to play till the seven years of age, then teach him good manners and politeness."[192] The Holy Prophet of Islam said:

"The child has three rights over its parents: 1. They select a good name for him/her. 2. Make him/her respectful (polite).3. Arrange a good spouse for him/her.[193]

The fondest hope of every parent will be that their children grow into polite and respectable persons. But this hope cannot be fullled

---

[186] Gharar al hukm, p. 34

[187] Gharar al hukm, p. 21

[188] Gharar al hukm, p. 242

[189] Gharar al hukm, p. 830

[190] Gharar al hukm, p. 293

[191] Gharar al hukm, p. 634

[192] Bihar al-anwar, v104, p. 95

[193] Wasail al-shiah, v 15, p. 123

without sincere and continued efforts. It will not be possible to infuse this trait in the children with sermonizing. The best route to this end is setting ideal example before the children by the parents with their exemplary behavior in their daily lives.

'Ali has said:

"Best behavior is that which you yourself start to practice."[194]

"Start instruction with oneself and then teach others. First make your character perfect and then sermon and advise others." [195]

Children are natural mimics. The capability to copy is very strong in their nature. The children imitate the ways of their parents and others around them. He will talk like them and he would try to walk like them. Instruction, off course, is a very important aspect of training, but it is not as strong as the capacity to mimic and learn, particularly in the early stages of childhood.

The parents, who are particular that their children should be polite and well behaved, must take special care to see that they are training them by personal examples. If the parents are polite to one another, naturally the children will follow suit.

The parents who themselves are devoid of politeness and good manners, should not expect good manners from their children. They might lecture the children hundreds of times on the norms of good behavior and politeness, but the children would be behaving under the experience of the attitude of the parents and others in the household. If the parents are impolite and abusive to each other, they will be setting a negative example to their growing children.

Children from such homes will be as bad mannered as the parents or, perhaps, more so. Any attempt at correcting them will fall on deaf ears. They will naturally think that the parents are asking them to do

---

[194] Gharar al hukm, p. 191

[195] Nahj ul balagha, v3, p. 166

what they themselves don't practice.

Example is always better than precept. But it is not right to think that lecturing will be totally ineffective. Good parents, who also set good example for their children, can always talk to them about the norms of good conduct and they will denitely accept their advice. This advice too has to be given with politeness.

There are parents who express their anger rather harshly when they notice the children doing something wrong. Sometimes they might say, "You naughty fellow Why didn't you wish the visitor? Why didn't you say 'Bi' to him? Are you dumb? Stupid and manner less child, why did you spread your legs impolitely in front of elderly visitors? Why were you noisy while visiting our friend's home You beast Why do you impolitely interrupt the conversation!"

These ignorant parents think that they are correcting their children with such talk. They don't know that good manners are not taught with bad manners. If the child is guilty of any indiscretion, he must be politely cautioned. There should not be others present at such sessions that should be conducted in a cool and friendly manner.

The Prophet of Islam used to greet the children and say, "I greet the children so that greeting becomes their habit."

Theft and Kleptomania

Several times it happens that a child spreads its hand to take something that is not his. He forcibly tries to take the eatables, fruits or toys of some other child. Stealthily takes away something from the pocket of the father or from the mother's purse. He takes sweets and other goodies from the pantry without the knowledge of his mother.

Picks up things stealthily from the shops visited by the family. Takes pencils, rubber etc of his siblings and school-mates without informing them. Several children do this sort of things in their childhood.

Seldom a person can be found who has never done such things in his childhood. Some parents are very upset nding their children doing such things and start imagining of a bleak future for the child. They feel that their child might turn into a thief or burglar when he grows up. With these pangs of remorse they keep worrying themselves.

First of all such parents should give their attention to the fact that they need not worry too much and feel sorry for the small aberration in the child. Lifting insignicantly small things by the child is not the sign that the child will turn into a thief in the future. They should know the child has not yet reached the stage to appreciate the rights of ownership of others, or to differentiate between what belongs to others and what is his own.

The child has subtly strong feelings and jumps to grab whatever attracts his attention. The child will not be naughty by nature but this attitude comes to him from outside inuences. These are all passing phenomena in his early life.

When he grows up, he might not do such things. There must be many pious, upright persons who might have done some unintentional stealing in their childhood. But the purpose of telling all this is not that the parents totally ignore reacting to the acts of theft of their children. I only wish to dispel their fears that the children might turn into thieves. Instead of lamenting over such incidents, they should discreetly try to correct the child.

A child of two to three years in particular is not able to distinguish between what belongs to him and what is not his. Whatever comes in his reach, he tries to take. Whatever is attractive to him, he wants to have.

At this stage shouting at the child and beating him will not be of any use. The best attitude for the parents will be to practically stop the child from doing such a thing if it happens in their presence. If the child tries to snatch something from another child, they should softly intervene. And despite all this, if the child takes the thing from the other child, the parents should restore it to the real owner as soon as they can.

The things that they don't want the child to handle, they should take care to keep them out of his reach. When the children reach a certain level of intelligence, they will start understanding about ownership of things. Now they will not try to grab others things. However, some children do continue the habit of stealing even after attaining the idea about ownership of things.

In such a situation the parents should not remain silent spectators.

They should not be complacent now, thinking that the child will automatically give up the habit. He might turn into a thief, or at least a kleptomaniac, who picks up things of others just for the heck of it, not knowing what he is doing. It is not right to ignore even if the child steals something belonging to his own parents

Some parents are so protective of their children that if someone reports that the child has stolen their things, they start wrongly defending their child. and blaming the other person of false accusation.

Such ignorant parents, with their negative attitude, unknowingly encourage the child to blatantly continue his stealing activity. The child will learn to steal and deny having done it.

Therefore the parents should not be unconcerned when they face such a situation. They should make efforts to stop the child from stealing and lying about it. There will be the risk of the bad habit taking root in his nature and making reform very difcult.

'Ali has said:

"Giving up habits is very difcult."[196]

At the rst instance the parents should try to remove the causes of the child wanting to steal. If the child needs pencil, paper or eraser; the parents should fulll this need. If they neglect this need of the child, it is likely that he will pick the things from his class-mates. He may even take money from the father's pocket to buy the things.

If the child wants a ball to play and the parents refuse to buy one for him, he might forcibly take the ball of a friend forcibly. Or even he might steal a ball from the neighborhood grocer. The parents must take care to fulll the child's needs to the extent possible.

If certain things he wants are beyond their means, they should make the child understand by telling him the facts affectionately. For example, they can tell him that they don't have so much money that

---

[196] Gharar al hukm, p. 181

they immediately buy for him the colour pencil box required urgently.

He may borrow the box today from his friend to do his immediate task and they shall get him one later. Tough attitude with the child might encourage him to steal. If the parents are keeping eatables locked in the pantry, the child will plan somehow to search the key and take out the goodies for eating. This thing can happen in the near impossible situation when the parents want to eat the things themselves and deny to the child.

When the parents hide away their money the child might get inclined to search for it. It is better the parents don't hide their cash from the children very much. They must take the children into their condence and should not give them a feeling that things are being hidden from them. They should teach the child that life is spent with some discipline. There are times for eating and they should not always keep munching things. Money is for buying necessities and should not be squandered carelessly.

Films of crime, theft and robbery should not be shown to the children. Story books and radio programs on such subjects should also be avoided. There are many instances that youth caught for crimes have confessed that they got the inspiration from movies for such acts.

The most important thing is that the parents and other members of the family try that the environment of their house is one of honesty and probity where others' ownership of things is respected. No one takes money from the parents' pockets and the things are not appropriated without the knowledge of the owner. Even the husband should not rummage the wardrobe of the wife without her knowledge. The parents also should respect the right of ownership of the children and should not handle their things without their consent.

The parents should not insult the child over his minor misdemeanors. They should not shout at him calling him names like cheat and thief. They should not threaten him that he would go to jail for his act of stealing. With such insults they cannot reform the child. He might, to the contrary, become stubborn and continue with his stealing. Or, perhaps in a revengeful mood he might commit bigger thefts.

The best method to save the situation for the parents would be to treat the child with discretion, love and softness. They should explain the grave consequences of stealing. They should convince him to return the stolen things to the owner and never repeat the act again.

But even after these attempts of reforming the child fail, then the only alternative will be to talk to him with a strong and forthright manner. Finally if the child proves totally incorrigible, they can reluctantly have recourse to physical punishment.

Jealousy

Jealousy or envy is a negative trait in human beings. A jealous person always envies others who are happy and comfortable. When he finds something good and attractive with others, he wishes that they lost the thing. Generally such a jealous person is neither capable of snatching away the good thing from the other person nor harm him in any way.

He continues to sulk and brood. He will be burning in the flames of jealousy day and night. An envious person is devoid of the pleasures and comforts of the world and the feelings of deprivation and the thought of the amenities enjoyed by others makes his own life miserable.

The Prophet of Islam has said:

"A jealous person is the unhappiest of his compatriots."[197] 'Ali, The Commander of the Faithful, says:

"Envy makes the life of a jealous person bleak."[198]

---

[197] Mustadrak al-wasail, v 2, p. 327

[198] Mustadrak al-wasail, v 2, p. 328

"An envious person never gets contentment and happiness."[199]

Jealousy has deleterious effects on the nerves and heart of a person and makes him sick and weak. 'Ali, The Commander of the Faithful, says:

"An envious person is always feeble and debilitated."[200]

Jealousy weakens the roots of the person's faith and turns him towards sin and disbelief. Lots of murders, ghts and other crimes are the result of envy and jealousy. Sometimes the envious person does backbiting of the person he is jealous of and spreads rumors and inappropriate designations about him. He sometimes causes damage to the properties of the other person.

Imam Muhammad al Baqir said:

"Envy destroys faith in the way re destroys the fuel."[201]

Jealousy is a part of the human nature. There will hardly be any persons who don't have this instinct. The Prophet of Islam says:

"There are three things no person is devoid of: base thoughts, bad actions, and jealousy."[202]

Therefore, this undesirable instinct must be curbed with all the force at the disposal of a person. It should not be allowed to ourish and grow. If the instinct of envy is allowed to persist, since it is a part of the person's nature, it would grow at leaps and bounds. It will reach such proportions that ghting it out will not be possible.

The best time when good manners are cultivated and the bad ones are eliminated is the childhood of a person. The element of jealousy too will be present in a child. The parents, with their own behavior, and proper attention to the child, can denitely cure the child of the

---

[199] Mustadrak al-wasail, v 2, p. 327

[200] Mustadrak al-wasail, v 2, p. 328

[201] Sha, v 1, p. 173

[202] al-mahajjatul bayda, v 3, p. 189

rudiments of the malady of jealousy that manifest in his behavior now and then.

If the parents treat all their children equitably, without any favoritism, the problem of one envying the other doesn't arise. The raiment, the food and other things in the use of the children should be of the same quality and standard. They should keep in mind equity in the matter of pocket money and general treatment of the children. They should not overtly compare the capabilities of the children in their presence, and even with others, if there is likelihood of the children learning about the comparison being made.

Such attitude can curb whatever degree of capability the weaker child has and might render him totally incompetent These well-meaning but ignorant parents think that they are training the child. To the contrary they aren't able to fulll their purpose and are adding fuel to the re. The innocent child's heart gets the ideas of jealousy and hate. He may get motivated to commit acts of enmity. There can always be the risk of his taking out spleen on his own siblings.

The parents should never compare their children with others'. They should never praise other children very much particularly in comparison with their own. It is not proper if the parents tell to their children, "How well behaved, polite and studious is our neighbor's son. How obedient he is and also he helps his mother with her work. His parents are really lucky to have a son like him." Such parents must understand that this type of comparison might hurt the ego of the child and have harmful implications.

The child, instead of mending his ways, may become adamant and revengeful.

The parents must strictly avoid comparing children. Some children are always more procient, better looking or smarter than others. It is possible that the parents may be more attached to one child than the others. There is no harm in this attitude. This is a normal human instinct. But in talk and actions they should not show any discrimination between the children.

They must ensure equitable treatment for all the children. If they desire to give any special treatment to a particular child, they should do it while other children are not around. Even if the parents are taking full care to give equitable treatment to all the children, the element of jealousy, which is instinctive in human nature, will still be present in the children to some extent. Every child wishes to be the darling of the parents and none other should have this privilege.

When he notices the parents expressing affection to the other siblings, he will feel momentary pang of jealousy. The child will slowly understand that he has to share the affection of the parents with the other brothers and sisters. The others too have a right over the parents. The parents, with discreet handling of the situation, can make the child accept the other brothers and sisters and thus prevent him from continuing with his feeling of envy.

If you nd that your son is envious of his brother or sister for some reason: he bullies them, pinches them, and uses harsh words with them, tries to deprive them of their shares of fruits and sweets, then he needs more of your attention. You should not close your eyes to these activities of the child.

You must impress on him that he is growing big and his little brother needs more attention than him. You must tell him that when he was a small kid like his little brother now, he too required and received more attention. Instead of trying to mend his ways strictly, impress on him that the little children are his own brothers and sisters. They too love him. If he didn't love them, who would? He must protect them if someone else tries to hurt them. Allah has given to him such lovely brothers and sisters, for which he must be thankful.

In conclusion it is necessary to mention that maintaining totally equitable treatment to all the children might be Utopian. How can the parents treat the son, the daughter, the elder and the younger the same way? The elder children can generally be given more freedom. But the younger ones have to be given more care. The elder ones will get more pocket money. The younger ones require more protection.

The sons are generally given more freedom of movement than the daughters. Therefore, keeping in mind the need for equity and freedom, the parents have to adopt different approach for the sons and the daughters. This treatment might give to the children some hard feelings. But if the parents properly explain to them that they have the same affection for all the children, but the norms of behavior for people differ according to the gender and age.

Although envy and jealousy are very undesirable traits in the eyes of Islam, and are in fact considered sins, the spirit of competition and rivalry are the components of efforts and struggle for human advancement. The difference between envy and rivalry is that a person becomes a rival of another person to match his achievements and to go ahead of him; but an envious person only feels jealous and is unable to compete and come forward. Rivalry in every eld of activity is a healthy phenomenon. The human civilization could have become stagnant without rivalry and competition.

One person writes:

"I had a sister two years elder to me. My parents used to love me more than her. Whatever I desired for, they used to give me. At every opportunity they used to praise me and totally neglected mention of my sister. My sister always used to nag me. Whenever she had a chance, she would beat and pinch me, call me names and break my favorite toys. She never wanted me to be happy for a moment. I used to think why my sister is troubling me so much? What wrong I have done to her?

She was very jealous of me and perhaps the partial behavior of the parents was reason for this rancor in her mind. The parents never realized that because of their partiality. My sister would try to take revenge on me. Now that my parents are no more, my sister is very kind with me. She feels very much if I have the slightest discomfort."

Anger

Anger and angst are a part of the human nature. They are present in the basic instinct of every person. This phenomenon rises from the heart and the mind of an individual. Then it assumes the shape of a ame and pervades the entire body. The eye and the visage become red, the limbs start shaking and froth comes forth from the mouth.

The senses escape out of the control of the person. The intelligence of the angry person disappears momentarily and in that condition there would be hardly any difference between him and a mad person. In this inebriated condition he might commit acts for which he would have to repent his entire life.

'Ali, The Commander of the Faithful, says:

"Keep away from anger because it starts with rage and ends in remorse.[203] Imam Ja'far as-Sadiq says:

"Anger is the key to all ills."[204]

Anger is also harmful to the piety and faith of the person. It can

---

[203] Mustadrak al-wasail, v 12, p. 326

[204] Usul al-Ka, v 2, p. 303

nullify his goo acts and make him a sinner.

The Prophet of Islam has said:

"Angst destroys the piety of a person as vinegar does destroy good honey."[205]

In a condition of frenzy a person utters unintelligent words and his actions are such that he becomes unpopular in the eyes of others.

'Ali, The Commander of the Faithful, says:

"Anger is a bad companion which exposes the failings of a person. It brings him closer to evil and takes him away from good."[206]

Perpetual anger affects the heart and the nerves of a person. And makes them debilitated and weak. Therefore, a person who is concerned about his reputation, health and piety he must ght the bad instinct of anger with full force at his command, lest it destroy his nerves, repute and faith.

It must also be borne in mind that anger is not unnecessary and harmful under all circumstances. At certain times its use is legitimate and advantageous. It must be used judiciously when the situation demands. This instinct only helps one protect his life and property from vandals and undesirable elements.

When the person has to protect his faith, his country or to defend the humanity in general, the instinct of anger will be a part of his chivalry. Without the presence of this instinct a person will be in the ranks of cowards who bow down their heads to any insults or ill treatment from others, If the instinct of anger remains in the control of the instinct of wisdom, it can be an asset for a person.

Fighting in the defense of one's country, the cause of one's faith (Amr bil Maroof nahi an-il Munkar), to protect one's family is legitimate. The instinct of angst makes one capable of taking part in such difcult

---

[205] Usul al-Ka, v 2, p. 302

[206] Mustadrak al-wasail, v 2, p. 326

tasks.

A pious and responsible Muslim will not remain a silent spectator to tyranny, injustice, dictatorship, perpetuation of sins, the forces of imperialism and colonialism etc. Islam permits its people to stand rmly and confront these forces with courage and equanimity, In such situation, however, the angst of the people, should not prevail over wise counsel. 'Ali, The Commander of the Faithful, says:

"If you become a follower of anger, it will take you towards destruction."[207]

This is not right to totally suppress the instinct of anger and make the human being insensitive, unconcerned and shameless. What is required is the need to avoid excessive and unnecessary expression of anger. This is possible with proper upbringing and grooming of the young persons.

Like the other instincts in a person, anger too is in its rudimentary form since the very childhood. The quantum of anger in a person is the reection of the upbringing he has received, and the environment he has been living in. If the parents maintain the instinct of anger at a moderate level in their affairs, the child too will learn to follow suit. The children of excitable and wrathful parents too will learn to be similar in their future lives.

The child sometimes shouts and rants in anger, his body shivers, the color of his face changes, he hits the ground with his feet, starts rolling on the oor, utters angry word and tries to go to a corner and hides himself. But all these antics of the child may not be all pranks. It can be in anger and the parents have to investigate the cause of the anger and try to remove it.

Anger denitely arises because of some worry or discomfort. Excessive pain, tiredness, sleeplessness, hunger, excessive thirst, cold and

---

[207] Mustadrak al-wasail, v 2, p. 226

heat make the child restless and give rise to anger. Doing things against the wish of the child, suppressing his freedom of movement, the feeling of undue attention to other children, feeding him forcibly can make the child restless and angry. Some parents teach the children in a subtle way to be angry. They shout at them and become unduly strict. If the child gets angry, they reciprocate with anger instead of trying to calm him down. The child thus gets trained to be a compulsively angry person.

If the child is hungry and thirsty, give him something to eat and drink. If he is tired, help him to sleep. If the child is angry because of your actions, try to amend them. If the anger of the child is because of some rambling thought, calm him down with sweet talk and lullabies. If the child is angry because he needs something, try to nd out his need and fulll it. When the child becomes normal, tell him that he need not cry and become angry to get something. Assure him that he has only to ask for the thing, and if the thing is good for him it will be given to him. Also warn him that if he cries and misbehaves in the future, his wishes may not be granted.

'Ali, The Commander of the Faithful, says:

"Beware of anger lest it dominates you and becomes a habit."[208]

Excitable children become angry at the slightest pretext because their nature is not strong. They are notable to tolerate any undesirable thing and get affected with the slightest disturbance and become angry.

---

[208] Gharar al hukm, p. 809

Tongue Lashing and Impertinence

Using bad words and talking impertinently is a very bad habit. The persons who do tongue lashing at whatever passes their mind, seldom stick to their word. They are very ckle of mind. They use bad words., keep nding fault with others for no rhyme or reason. They keep causing hurt to others with their irresponsible talk.

Using bad words is *haram* and is considered a major sin. The Prophet of Islam has said:

"Allah has forbidden Heaven to the users of foul language. There is also curse on those who abuse, are shameless and impertinent and they will all be denied entry to Paradise. .Whatever a foul mouthed person says about others, he does it thoughtlessly and never bothers about what opinion others have of him."[209]

Imam Ja'far as-Sadiq says:

"Swearing, bad-mouthing and impertinence are the signs of hypocrisy (nifaaq) and faithlessness."[210] Allah says in the Holy The Holy Qur'an:

---

[209] Usul al-Ka, v 2, p. 323

[210] Usul al-Ka, v 2. p. 325

"Shame on all such persons who talk about the failings of others and indulge in ridiculing them." (The Holy Qur'an, 104:1)

Foul mouthed persons are generally inferior and petty minded. They make others enemies with indiscreet talk. People abhor them. They try to keep away from them and avoid their company.

The Prophet of Islam has said:

"Among people the worst is one whose talk is not liked by others and they try to avoid meeting him."[211] Imam Ja'far as-Sadiq says:

"When people don't like to even listen to the talk of a person, his destiny will be Hell!"[212] The Prophet has said:

"A Mu'min (pious person) will not be taunting, doesn't criticizing, blaming and talking ill of others."[213]

The child by nature is not capable of bad mouthing. He may learn this from his parents, brothers, sisters and friends at school or play. But the maximum effect will be of the attitude of the parents. The parents can be the most effective example for the children. The parents not only are responsible for their own behavior but have the very important responsibility of training their children properly.

These are the parents alone who either make the children polite and gentle or impertinently loud mouthed. Some parents, either in jest or in anger call bad words with their children. This way they inadvertently give a wrong training to the children. There are some homes where the use of the bad words is a common practice.

'Son of a dog', 'mother of a dog', 'fool', 'idiot', 'senseless donkey', 'animal', 'shameless' and several others are the appellations thrown at

---

[211] Usul al-Ka, v 2, p. 325

[212] Usul al-Ka, v 72, p. 327

[213] al-mahajjat ul bayda, v 3, p. 127

one another in such households either in jest or right earnest anger.

The parents, whose duty it is to prevent the foibles of their children, themselves are perpetrating such wrong acts and encouraging the children to follow their example. They thoughtlessly abuse each other and call names in front of the children.

The parents taunt the children and use unethical language with them. How can such parents expect that their child will grow into a gentle and respectable adult. They should realize that the child might prove even worse than themselves. They should remember that sooner or later they will nd the child trading the same idiom that he has been hearing again and again from his parents. Then any amount of sermonizing and beatings cannot reform the child. The best remedy is that the parents reform themselves in good time before it gets too late.

Many a time the children learn this bad habit from their companions. The parents should keep their eyes and ears open to such behavior in their children and nip the defect in the bud. They should ask their children to try to avoid meeting such children very much.

If you ever nd your child uttering any abusive word, then don't just smile and keep quiet. With shouting and threats too such situations cannot be handled. This method might backre. The best way to correct the child is to talk softly with the child and explain to him about the ill effects of using bad words.

Backbiting or Carrying Words

Backbiting is a very bad habit, and unfortunately it is very much prevalent in the society. If someone speaks something against someone, the backbiter carries the word to the other person saying that so- and-so was saying such-and-such a thing about you. Carrying words are signs of meanness and evil.

This creates chasms between good friends. Many crimes, skirmishes, enmities, murders and feuds are the result of misunderstandings between people due to backbiting. The peace of many households gets shattered due to this nasty practice. Husbands and wives are separated, friends become enemies, parents turn against their children mainly because of the backbiting by some nasty, thoughtless persons.

When a backbiter gets exposed, he will be thrown out from everywhere and people hate to see his face. The people curse the backbiter and wish him destruction. The worst of backbiting is the act of sleuthing for the evil tyrants. If someone does eves-dropping for a tyrant and a pious person unnecessarily comes into trouble because of this, and suffers bodily damage or death due to torture, then the backbiter will be equally answerable as that evil person who engaged him to do the nefarious job. They will both be punished on the Day of Judgment. Although, in this case, the back-biter was not directly involved with the physical act of torturing the innocent person.

The Prophet of Islam says:

"The worst person is one who does backbiting against his Muslim brother to the King and do sleuthing against him. This sleuthing is bad for him, for the friend against whom he had reported and also for the King."[214]

Islam has pronounced the act of sleuthing and backbiting *haram* and there are many traditions of the Prophet and others in this regard.

Imam Muhammad al Baqir says:

"The backbiter will be denied entry to the Heaven."[215] 'Ali, The Commander of the Faithful, says:

"The foul and evil amongst you are those who do backbiting and create differences between friends and expose the defects of good people."[216]

There can be many reasons for backbiting. Sometimes enmity becomes the cause of the act. The backbiter may be inimical to one of the parties and be jealous of their good relations. He keeps giving false and malicious reports about one to the other till they fall into his trap. Sometimes the backbiter, as a force of habit, transmits a false and damaging information about one person to the other creating serious differences between them. In this instance the backbiter doesn't have any ulterior motive except to satisfy his urge to carry a tail. The Religion of Islam has forbidden even to give ear to backbiting.

The Prophet says:

"Neither should you do backbiting, nor listen to a back biter."[217]

---

[214] Bihar al-anwar, v 75, p. 266

[215] Usul al-Ka, v 2, p. 369

[216] Usul al-Ka, v 2, p. 375

[217] Majma al zawaid, v 8, p. 91

'Ali, The Commander of the Faithful, says:

"Refute the talk of the backbiter and the one who is unduly inquisitive."[218]

It is evident that if no one takes cognizance of the talk of the backbiter, then he will stop doing it. Whoever carries words to you about others, you must be sure that he is not your friend. If he was really your friend he would have defended you while others talked against your interest.

If someone tells something in condence, a good Muslim never speaks about it to others. He will keep control over his tongue and never try to sleuth around. Many persons pick up the offending habit of backbiting from their childhood. It is a reection of what they see and hear happening around them.

Therefore the parents shoulder a big responsibility that they protect their children from getting the nefarious habit of backbiting. First, the parents themselves should refrain from talking ill of others. The mother should not report of some acts of her neighbour and other relations .to the father.

The father too should not speak to the mother against his friends and acquaintances. Because, if the parents have the habit of speaking ill of others behind their backs, the children too will indulge in such talk.

Sometimes a child speaks to his father against her mother and the elder sister. In such instances the duty of the father is to correct the child and tell him that it is not good to backbite. He should tell him that if want to say something about your mother or sister, tell directly to them. What you are doing is backbiting, which is very bad. If the children try to backbite, totally ignore them at the moment and try to talk on some other interesting subject.

---

[218] Gharar al hukm, p. 145

The Prophet of Islam has said:
"Don't give your ears to the backbiter !"[219]

---

[219] Gharar al hukm, p. 125

Fault-Finding

Criticizing others and finding faults in them for no reason is one of the worst habits of human beings. People hate the persons who habitually keep on finding fault with others. They try to avoid such troublesome persons. Sometimes this faultfinding becomes the cause of enmity and conflict. If someone's faults are mentioned when he is not around, it is termed as backbiting (*ghaibat*) and even if this is done in the presence of the person, it is an affront and not desirable. The Religion of Islam has termed *ghaibat* as a major sin. There are many traditions on the subject. For example:

The Prophet of Islam, delivering a sermon, has said in a pronounced tone:

"Those people Who profess to be believers with their tongues; but the faith has not entered their hearts Don't ever do backbiting and criticism of the Muslims and don't keep searching their faults. Because one who tries to find his brother's faults Allah will bare his own faults and render him the laughing stock for others."[220]

Imam Ja'far as-Sadiq says:

---

[220] Jam'i al sa'da, v 2, p. 203

"Whoever says something injurious to the reputation of a Mu'min, Allah shall remove him from the group of His friends and send to the band of Satan who too will refuse to accept him as a friend."[221]

The Prophet of Islam said:

Whoever does *ghaibat* of any believer man or woman, Allah will not accept his prayer (*salat*) and fasting (*sawm*) for forty days, unless he obtains the pardon of those whose backbiting he has done."[222]

Imam Ja'far as-Sadiq said:

"*Ghaibat* and faultnding are taboo. And they destroy the virtues of a person as the re destroys the fuel."[223]

Unfortunately such a major sin has become an everyday routine for our people. It has reached such grave proportions that the people don't consider that they are sinning backbiting and nding faults in others. The mother criticizes the father and the father nds fault with her. Neighbors and relatives don't tire counting each other's faults. The innocent children pick up this loathsome habit from their home and parents. Children do backbiting of other children. When they grow up doing this, it becomes difcult to shun the bad habit.

Some parents pamper and praise their children to the sky. While, in fact, they need to gloss over their shortcomings. Sometimes the parents falsely praise the child for the things he has not achieved to put him to ridicule for his failures.

In such situations the children might turn hostile to the parents. Or even they may get the habit of uttering blatant falsehoods. They can also become the victims of inferiority complex. It is better, therefore, for the parents not to unnecessarily talk of the failures of the children derisively.

---

[221] Jam'i al sa'da, v 2, p. 305

[222] Jam'i al sa'da, v 2, p. 304

[223] Jam'i al sa'da, v 2, p. 305

Children's Quarrels

One matter of some concern is the differences and ghts between children at homes. When a family has more than one child, there is likelihood of ghts. One thinks that the other is usurping his privileges and has unnecessarily come to share things with him. They push each other around and grab toys from each other.

When they start going to school they dirty each other's note-books and other things. They make fun of each other. When one tries to concentrate on his school assignment, the other makes noises to disturb him. Every child knows the pranks that he can play on his brothers and sisters.

In this situation the parents are the helpless spectators. The complaints about the ghts reach them. The difculty comes for them when sometimes the parents get involved to arbitrate in the quarrels of the children. The mother tells the father that he doesn't give attention to the upbringing of the children. They don't fear you. It is your careless attitude that the house is literally an arena for ghts.

The father complains to the mother that if she were a careful person, the children wouldn't have turned so naughty as they are. It is her support that encourages the children to misbehave.

Here the parents should remember that the children are, after all, children They cannot be expected to sit quietly in a corner like old persons. You must accept the fact that children's ghts are a natural phenomenon. Even the elders sometimes do ght. How can the children be expected to sit quietly all the while. Children are generally mischievous. Playing pranks at one another they might ght. But soon they get together and forget the differences. They cannot remain away from each other carrying long faces.

One psychologist says:

"This is an important matter that we should never think that in a house where there are many children there prevails perpetual peace amongst them; the children live amicably, never ght for once Whichever child we have talked to, said that Mom and Dad expect them to live amicably without ghting with one another. But if you give a serious thought to the matter, the trend of the children ghting with one another is not such a big problem."[224]

We should also know that the habit of the children ghting with one another would disappear as they grow in age. If the parents accept the ghts between children as a temporary and natural phase, then they would not worry about it so much.

Another psychologist says:

"Lots of activities of the children like playing pranks on one another, ghting and wrestling with one another will taper off with passage of time."[225]

Yes, it is right that most parents cannot completely eliminate the ghts between their children. But with tact and clever handling they can reduce their frequency and intensity. The careful parents never remain spectators when the children ght. They intervene tactfully

---

[224] Ruwan shinasi kudak, p. 286

[225] Ruwan shinasi kudak, p. 286

and ensure that the children don't cause bodily harm to each other during ghts.

They have rst to investigate the cause of the ght and try to eliminate it. One main cause of the differences between the children is the feeling of jealousy. It is necessary that the reason for the jealousy springing up in the child is detected and a remedy found.

A child wants all the attention for himself. He doesn't like to share the affections of the parents with other children. The rst born is generally pampered by the parents. But when the second arrives, the conditions are changed. Naturally the parents have to divide their attention and have to give the major share to the smaller child. Now the elder child starts getting the feeling of insecurity. He starts feeling neglected.

He feels the new arrival is an uninvited guest who is holding the attention and care of his beloved parents. He becomes envious of the baby, but knows that he has to tolerate him because the parents are showering love on him. In such situations the elder child sometimes malingers, pretending illness, to keep the attention of the parents concentrated on him. Sometimes he may fall on the oor, refuse to eat food, cry and try other pretences to attract the parents' attention.

Such a child considers himself deprived and develops a sort of hatred for his other siblings. He awaits an opportunity to wreak revenge on them. The parents have to discreetly avoid such situations arising. They should prepare the children to receive the new arrival before he is born. They must tell the children that their little sibling is expected soon. When it will grow up, it will play with them and love them. When they prepare something for the new-born, they should give some gifts to the elder children too, so that they don't feel neglected.

When the mother gets admitted to a maternity home for delivery, the father should give some gifts to the children at home so that their minds are diverted and they don't miss the mother. The father should tell them on the occasion that the gifts are given to them to celebrate the arrival of the little one He should ask them that when the little one came home, they should not make much noise. The parents should not praise the baby too much in the presence of the other children. They should give a little more attention to the older children to give them the feeling of assurance that the new one is not come to deprive them of their parents attention.

'Ali, The Commander of the Faithful, says:

"Justice removes differences and promotes friendship."[226] "Just treatment is always the best strategy."[227]

It is always possible that some of the children might have special qualities that become the darlings of the parents. Some children may be more intelligent, some more pretty and some other more polite to deserve special attention of the parents. One child might perform excellently at school and attract lot of praise from the parents.

These extraordinary expressions of love because of some special quality in a child will not be anything out of the ordinary. But excessive repetition of such praises is not advisable.

Some parents, as a strategy to promote competition between their children, talk about the good qualities of one to the other(s). For example, they may say, ' Hasan Work hard at studies that you get high grades in your examinations as did Abbas!' They say, ' Zainab, you must help your mother for his household chores as Zahra' is so nicely doing!' ' Ridha', observe good table manners like your brother, 'Ali. What a polite and courteous boy he is!'

This attitude of the parents is not right. It might not bring about positive and desirable results. To the contrary, it might create hard feelings and jealousy between brothers and sisters. They may become

---

[226] Gharar al hukm, p. 64

[227] Gharar al hukm, p. 64

revengeful and might themselves indulge in unnecessary comparisons between each other.

Another very important reason for the ghts between the children is the high expectations of the parents from them. The child wants to play with the toys of his sibling; the parents prohibit him from doing it. This gives rise to the ght between the two. At this juncture the parents intervene. First they quietly try to convince the children to become quiet. If the quarrel still persists, they ask the other child to give its toy to the one who wants to borrow it for playing. They tell him that it is they who have brought the toy for him. The toy is not his property. If he still refused to give the toy to his brother, they would not love him nor bring any more toys for him.

The child becomes helpless and parts with his toy. But he starts thinking that the parents are tyrannical and the brother is bad. He develops hatred in his heart for both. He will express this hatred whenever there is an opportunity. This is quite natural that the child was thinking that the toys were his own and that none other had a right to play with them.

Without his consent. He thinks that he is the victim of the tyranny of his parents and the other brother. In the circumstance, the child is right. Because, in the rst instance they don't permit the other siblings to play with the toys they had given to him. The thoughtful parents try to create a spirit of co-operation between their children. They must have an amicable atmosphere that they share all their toys and games with each other.

Sometimes the reason for differences cropping up between the children is that the parents entrust one task to a particular child and leave the others with nothing to do. This situation can give rise to ghts. To avoid such situations the parents should try to make the children busy with something or other. Then they will not have a feeling of neglect.

Sometimes even ghts between the parents encourage the children to follow suit. When the innocent children see that the parents are compulsive ghters, they start thinking that ghts are a way of life. In emulation of the parents they start looking for reasons to commence ghting.

Therefore, the parents who are fed up of the constant ghts between their children, should do introspection and reform themselves. Then they must turn their attention to set the children right. There will hardly be any family that has no difference of opinion amongst its members. But if the parents take care not to air their differences in the presence of the children, the children will not be encouraged to argue and ght. But, even then if there are some minor ghts between the children, the parents must discreetly intervene and sort out the matter to the satisfaction of all.

In the end we would like to caution you that in spite of observing all the cautions, your family may not be totally free of ghts between the children. After all children are human, and the instinct to ght is there in every individual. In fact the children are generally hyperactive and ghting can be a way of dissipating some of their energy. The parents must exercise care that when the children ght, they don't cause bodily harm to one another and the property around them. They should not worry too much if some children have more inclination to ght. This is a transient habit and it tapers off with time.

Friends and Friendship

A good friend and companion is the greatest gift of God. In adversity, a friend only is the refuge for a person and solace for his heart and soul. In this world, that is full of hardships and hurdles, presence of a true friend is absolutely necessary for every individual. One who doesn't have any friend, will be like a person, all alone, away from home. He will not have anyone to commiserate with him in the times of need.

Imam Musa ibn Ja'far was asked what is the ideal source for comfort in this world. The Imam replied: "An airy house and plenty of friends!"[228]

Imam 'Ali says:

"The weakest person is one who cannot make anyone his friend and brother."[229] "Not having friends is like being a stranger in ones own land and being a loner."[230]

---

[228] Bihar al-anwar, v 74, p. 177

[229] Bihar al-anwar, v 74, p. 154

[230] Bihar al-anwar, v 74, p. 179

As the grown ups need friends, the children too want friends and companions. A child who doesn't have friends, will always be lonely and forlorn. The child, by nature, needs a friend and companion. He cannot be denied this natural need. There is also a subtle difference between a friend and acquaintance.

Perhaps, a child may have acquaintances but no friends. Sometimes a child selects a friend from his class fellows and the children in his neighborhood. The cause for picking up a particular person as a friend may not be evident. Perhaps the spiritual similarity between the two has brought them together.

The Commander of the Faithful, 'Ali, says:

"The hearts of people are like migrant nomads, whosoever loves them, they are attached to him."[231]

A friend cannot be thrust on anyone. The parents cannot very much restrict the child to accept particular persons as friends. The child must be free to make his own choice of friends. But this freedom will be with some conditions and restrictions. The character and conduct of the friends will have to be observed by the parents before they permit the child to pick a friend. If a child selects a courteous and polite friend, he will denitely benet by picking up his good habits. To the contrary, if the friend has undesirable habits then, naturally, the child will take to some of his bad habits. There are plenty of children and youths fallen into the morass of sin because of indiscreetly selecting bad friends. .

The Prophet of Islam has said:

"A man follows the faith, ways and habits of his friend."[232] 'Ali, The Commander of the Faithful, says:

"The most fortunate are those who have connections with good

---

[231] Bihar al-anwar, v 74, p. 178

[232] Usul al-Ka, v 72, p. 375

people."²³³

This is the reason the Religion of Islam exhorts its peoples to abstain from bad company. 'Ali said:

"Avoid making friendship with transgressors and sinning persons because evil creates evil."²³⁴ Imam Zain ul Abidin told to his son, Imam Muhammad al Baqir:

"O My son Avoid acquaintance of ve type of persons: 1. Don't be friends with a liar. He will be like a mirage. He will trick you. When a thing is far, he will say it is near; and when it is at hand, he will say that it is very far. 2. Don't make a transgressor and sinner your friend because he might sell you for as low a price. 3. Don't make a parsimonious and stingy person your friend who may not help you in times of need. 4. Don't make a stupid person your friend, lest he bring harm to you with his stupidity. It is possible that with all good intentions, he might bring harm to you with his foolish actions. 5. Don't be friend with those who deprive their kin of their rights. Such persons are shorn of Allah's Blessings and are accursed people."²³⁵

Responsible and thoughtful parents will not be totally unconcerned with the type of friends their children cultivate. While the parents must know the type of friends a child has, they should not appear to be interfering in their personal matters.

If the parents can provide a good friend to their child, they have made a great contribution to his virtuous future. But this is not such an easy task. The best way is to acquaint the child with what is good, and what is not, when he comes to the age of understanding. They should explain to the child the defects that might be there in undesirable friends.

---

[233] Gharar al hukm, p. 189.

[234] Bihar al-anwar, v 74, p. 199

[235] Usul al-Ka, v 72, p. 376

The parents must keep a subtle watch over the activities of the child and his friends from a distance. If they nd that the friends are good, they must appreciate them. They should create opportunities for the child to meet such friends. But if they notice that the child has picked up an undesirable acquaintance, then they should discreetly try to cut this friendship short. If the child persists in such friendship, deal with the matter strictly.

The parents can help the child in making good friends by another method. They should pick children in their neighborhood with good behavior, character and background. Create opportunities for the children to meet and react with one another. If they become friends, encourage them to cement the friendship. This way, even if there are some minor defects in their own child, they can be warded off in the company of good children. For example, if a child is timid, he might overcome his timidity by being friends with a bold and courageous child.

The parents should not be totally oblivious of the type of friends their child has. Particularly when the child is on the threshold of youth. This will be the period in his life when habits take root. .Any negligence on the part of the parents might result in irreparable harm to the character and conduct of the child, if he persists to be in bad company. They should remember the dictum: Prevention is better than cure!

'Ali, The Commander of the Faithful, says:

"For everything there is a calamity, and for virtue the calamity is a bad friend." One gentleman writes:

"My parents never permitted me to meet my friends. If sometimes friends visited me, I tried to send them away quickly after talking with them for a while. One friend of mine used to live very near our home. My parents knew him well but never allowed us to visit each other. I used to wish to have friends, meet them, chat and play with them.

But my parents were the impediment. I was very sad about this. One day I had decided to visit my friend, whatever camel told my Mom that I had to go for my exams. I took permission for going to attend the examination but, in fact, I made a beeline to my friend's house. This friend's house was at a little distance from our home. I boarded an omnibus and reached his place. There were other children too at my friend's place. We had lots of fun together, When I returned home in the evening, Mom asked me why I was so late. To hide one lie, I had to utter another.

Now I wonder if Mom was not aware that the children too need friends and companions. Why did they restrict me so much?!'

One girl writes:

"Once I invited some friends home. I had some savings from my pocket money. With this money I ran to the neighborhood grocery and brought a pack of ice cream. My mother was away visiting some people.

While my friends were eating the ice cream, Mom returned home. I was very scared that she might scold me. She didn't bother a bit about my feelings and said angrily to my friends,' You girls are making Saima waste her money!'

My friends abruptly went away. My Mom didn't stop at this. She visited my school the next day and complained to our class teacher that my friends visit our home and encourage me to waste my money. She told the teacher that the girls visited a day earlier and asked me to buy ice cream for them.

My friends, who were also my class fellows, said, 'Aunty We shall pay you the price of the ice cream we ate at your home yesterday' I felt so ashamed and belittled that I wished the earth went asunder and I fell into the abyss. Ever since that day, I had never gone to the school. All my friends progressed in their studies. Today I am a forlorn and lonely person, lagging behind in all walks of life."

The Child and Theological Education

The human beings are instinctively attracted towards God and religion. The fountainhead of this instinct is the human nature.

Allah says in the Holy Book:

"Then set thou thy face uprightly for (the right) religion, in natural devotion to the truth(following) the nature caused by God in which He hath made the people." (The Holy Qur'an, 30:30)

Every child, by nature, is a worshipper of God, but the inuence of the external environment might bring about change in this condition; as the Prophet of Islam has said:

"Every child is born with Islamic Nature, but later on the parents might make him a Jew, a Christian or a Zoroastrian."[236]

It is the responsibility of the parents to give birth to their child in such an environment that the naturally endowed instinct of Religion

---

[236] Bihar al-anwar, v 3, p.281

in him is properly nourished. The day a child comes into this world, he is attracted towards the Power that will provide him his needs. But the child will not have his understanding developed to an extent to express anything about the Focus of its attention.

But, in stages, the understanding dawns on the child. A child, who gets his upbringing in a religious family, starts recognizing Allah from around the age of four years. This is the age when different questions start cropping up in the mind of a child. Sometimes he utters the name of Allah. His questions indicate that his nature is awake and is keen to gather more and more information:

The child thinks about:

- Who made the sun?
- Who has created the moon and the stars?
- Does Allah love me?
- Does Allah like sweet things?
- Who brings the rain?
- Who gave birth to Dad?
- Is Allah listening to our talk?
- Can we talk with Allah over the 'phone?
- Where does Allah live?
- How is His face?
- Does Allah live in the skies?

From the age of four years the child starts to think of thousands of such questions. It is evident from these questions that the instinct of Godliness is awakening in the child. By asking these questions he tries to quench his thirst for knowledge. It is not known, at that tender age, what opinion the child has of Allah. He perhaps thinks that Allah is like his Dad, but is denitely bigger and more powerful. As the child grows, his understanding of Allah too grows.

The parents shoulder a big responsibility at this stage. They have to play a very critical role in shaping the beliefs of their child. If the parents are a little negligent at this stage, then they will be subject to heavy retribution on the Day of Judgment. They must try to carefully answer all the questions their little child asks. If they avoid answering the questions for some reason, they might cause the extinction of the child's urge for discovery. But it may not be easy to answer all the questions of the child. The answers shall have to be correct, short and narrated in simple words.

As the child grows, he will become capable of understanding more difcult information. The parents will have to prepare themselves to reply to the probable questions that the child might ask them. They should not give to the child any information that might be beyond his comprehension. Such answers might confuse the child instead of quenching his thirst for knowledge. The Theological education of the child should be such that he is able to grasp with ease. Imam Ja'far as-Sadiq says:

"When the child is three years old, teach him to say 'La ilaha illal Lah' (There is no god, but Allah). Then leave him alone. When he is three years, seven months and twenty days; teach him to say Muhammad ar Rasool Allah (Muhammad is the Prophet of Allah). Leave him alone till he completes four years of age. Now teach him to say the *salawat* (the praises) of the Prophet (and his holy progeny)."[237]

Make the children learn to recite simple couplets about religious matters. This will be an interesting exercise for them. Then teach them about the Nubbuwat (the Prophethood) and Imamat (the Vicegerency). First the child must be told about the Prophet that he has been sent by Allah for the guidance of mankind.

Then they must be told about the Prophet's superior qualities and

---

[237] Makarim al akhlaq, v 1, p. 254

his exemplary way of life. Narrate to the child some interesting events of the Prophet's life. Then the child must be told about the Vicegerents of the Prophet for the continuity of the correct guidance of his people after him. All this information should be conveyed to the child in the form of short narrations to retain his continued interest.

About Qiyamat (the Doomsday) a child does not give early attention. He thinks that he and his parents will live happily forever. Talking to a child about death at that tender age may not be desirable. The child thinks that the people who died have gone on a long journey. Sometimes tragedies do take place in the families while the children are still small. In these circumstances the parents have to discreetly broach the subject of death with them. If, unfortunately, the child's Grandpa is dead, he might ask, ' Mom Where did Grandpa go?'

In such situations the facts must be explained to the child. The child can be told that his grand parent is no more. He has gone to the Other World. Every one who dies, goes to that World. If he were a good person in this life, he would rest in the Heaven where there are beautiful gardens. If the person who has died was a bad person in this life, he would go to the Hell which is full of re. The child should be informed about the inevitability of death slowly. He must be told that this life is transient and everyone has to go to the Other World.

This informal instruction of the religious knowledge should continue till the child completes his primary, middle and higher levels of schooling.

The Child and the Religious Duties

It is true that the boys attain the age of responsibility (*baligh*) at fteen and the girls at age nine. This is the age when the juridical norms become mandatory for them. But the performance of religious duties may not be postponed till the child reaches the age of responsibility. They must be encouraged to perform the religious duties from early childhood so that when they become compulsory, they would already be in the habit of fullling them.

Fortunately, in families of religious people, a child starts to emulate its parents performing the religious rites. Sometimes he spreads the prayer carpet for the parents, sometimes he puts down his head to the ground in supplication with the parent. He repeats Allah o Akbar (God is Great) and La ilaha illa Lah with his parents. He will recite small religious couplets with his mother.

The thoughtful parents make good use of this natural instinct of the child to emulate. If a child does these things, the parents give him a smile of appreciation. There should not be an element of force in making the child learn the religious rites.

The parents should not start formal teaching of the religious rites in early childhood. At the age of ve the child can learn to recite the

Sura al Fatiha (The Opening) of the Holy The Holy Qur'an. This has to be done slowly in several days to keep the interest of the child in learning to do the recitation.

At the age of seven the child should be asked to offer regular prayers. The parents should themselves set an example to the child by offering all the ve prayers, regularly and punctually, at their appointed times. At the age of nine years make it binding on the children to offer regular prayers.

They should explain to the children that the prayers are mandatory when they are home and also when they travel. If the child abstains from praying, the parents should deal with him strictly. If the parents are themselves regular at offering their prayers, they can easily make the children habituated of following suit.

When the children reach the age of responsibility, they will already be regular at offering the mandatory prayers. If the parents take the excuse that the child is still too small, and they would teach him to pray when he comes of age, then it would be very difcult to initiate the child into regular prayers. It is a common belief that old habits are difcult to change. This is the reason that the Prophet of Islam and the Holy Imams have asked the parents to initiate the children to offer prayers from the six or seven years of age.

Imam Muhammad al Baqir says:

"We encourage our children start praying from the age of ve years and at seven years we order them to pray ve times a day regularly. "[238]

The Prophet of Islam has said:

"When your children are six years old, order them to offer the prayers. When they are seven, ask them more strictly to be regular at prayers. If necessary, they must be punished if they don't become

---

[238] Wasail al-shiah, v 3, p. 12

regular in their prayers."²³⁹

Imam Muhammad al Baqir or Imam Ja'far as-Sadiq has said: "When the child is seven years old, then ask him to wash his face, the feet and the hands before offering prayers. But when he is nine years old, teach him the correct method of doing the Wudhu' (the mandatory ablutions prior to offering prayers). This is the time when the child is strictly instructed to offer regular prayers."²⁴⁰

Imam Ja'far as-Sadiq says:
"When a child is six years old, then it is necessary he learns to offer prayers and if he is physically capable he must also be encouraged to fast during the month of *Ramadhan*."²⁴¹

The child should be initiated slowly to fasting during *Ramadhan*. A child who is physically t for fasting should be woken up at the time of *sahr* (the meal before sunrise), so that he eats at this time instead of the breakfast at the regular morning times. If the child is keen to fast the whole day, encourage him to complete it.

But, if during the day, the child feels uneasy, he may be permitted to break his fast before time. The number of fasts by the child may be increased gradually. When the child reaches the age of understanding, he must be instructed that offering regular prayers ve times a day and fasting on all days during the month of *Ramadhan* is mandatory.

If he is irregular in his compliance of these, he would be a sinner and liable to punishment by God. The parents must explain to the child the advantages and the rewards of fasting during *Ramadhan*. This will give more courage to the child to do the fasting.

During the last days of Ramadhan, make other duties lighter for the child. He must be allowed more hours of rest during the day. At

---

[239] Mustadrak al-wasail, v 1, p. 171

[240] Wasail al shiah, v 3, p. 13

[241] Wasail al shiah, v 3, p. 12

the end of the fasting period, the child must be given some gift as an encouragement for his efforts. During the fasting period the parents should take care that the children don't try to eat something hidden from others' view.

It is necessary for the parents to instruct the children at the proper time about the wet-dreams they get at puberty. They must be instructed about doing the *ghusl* (the mandatory cleansing bath after having an emission) and *istinja* (the washing of the genitals with water after urinating).

It is necessary to remind here that if they wish their children to be regular visitors to the mosques and religious symposia, then they must put them into the habit from their childhood. They should take them to the mosque and the places of religious discourses. These visits will create interest in the children for going to the congregations.

In the end, it will not be out of place to remind that before reaching the age of understanding it is not mandatory on the child to observe the compulsory religious rites. If he is unable to perform certain rites at certain times, he is not committing any transgression. But it will not be proper for the parents to leave the children totally independent to do whatever they wish to. The child must be told that if in his innocence he causes any physical or bodily harm to others, he shall have to pay the Deeth (the ne for harming others) when he reaches the age of understanding.

On the other hand if the child is left free without any checks whatsoever, he might get into the habit of committing sins and wrong acts. The dictum is: 'Old habits die hard' The habits cultivated during the childhood remain with the person, however much one tries to banish them. Therefore it is necessary for the parents to instruct the children about the dos and don'ts from their very early days. They must stop them from doing taboo acts and encourage them to do good deeds.

Political and Social Training

Today's children are the youth of tomorrow. They will run the affairs of the society in the future. Their awareness and understanding of the political compulsions of the country will be of great importance. They will be the keepers of the cultural and economic wealth of the nations. They will have to strive maintaining and advancing the greatness of their homeland.

They will have to face the imperialist aggressors and ght against their machinations. The children should therefore be groomed from their early days to be ready to serve their country. The greatest responsibility will rest on the shoulders of the parents to groom their children properly.

The foundation for the political and sociological training has also to be laid in the childhood of a person. By the time a child reaches the stage of youth, he should be aware of the social and political problems of the community in which he lives. He should be made aware of the poverty and backwardness rampant in his country. The good qualities and failings of the rulers of the day have to be informed to the child who is on the threshold of youth.

They should be told about the lacunae in the running of the society.

He should know the general conditions prevailing in the towns and the countryside. The child may still not have the adult franchise and he cannot cast his vote. But the parents must explain to him the purpose of the election and the conduct thereof. They should also explain to him as to how to select the best candidate from the list of persons contesting in that area.

The parents must give the child their own example that they voted for a particular candidate because of certain qualities he has. The child can attend the election meetings and processions. He can join in raising slogans. He may distribute leaets of the candidate he thinks is deserving of being elected. This work will give boost to his awareness.

The Iranian Revolution has proved that the children and youth can contribute meaningfully in the political process of a country. They were the youth who, with their slogans, meetings, protests and active participation made the oppressive regime surrender. They relieved the oppressed people of Iran from the clutches of the agents of the tyrannical Shah's minions. The world knows that the Iranian Revolution succeeded because of the supreme sacrices made by the youth of the nation.

It is necessary that the children study the political situation of their country, in particular, and of the world, in general. They can do this by cultivating the habit of reading a good newspaper everyday. The can also watch and listen to the news bulletins on the television and the radio. They can also have group discussions with their parents and friends. This way they can develop interest in the welfare of their countrymen and themselves. This process will help the child develop good political and social awareness.

The future of the country, no doubt, will be in their hands and the hands of myriad other youths of the land. The children should know that the worldly life cannot be separated from the Hereafter, and, similarly, the Faith from the political process also could never be separated. The youth of the country should be actively associated with the political and social happenings of the country. The youth must be given more freedom of choice to participate in the political process of the nation.

The Child and the Radio and Television

The radio, television and cinema are very useful inventions. They can be very good tools for training and education. The tenets of faith and moral values can be propagated through these media. The thoughts of the people can be sharpened by means of these mediums. Information on agricultural and industrial developments could be disseminated through them. Awareness on the aspects of health and sanitation can be popularized through these media.

Man can derive innumerable benets from the electronic media. But while they have advantages, they have many disadvantages for the society too.

When these media fall into the hands of irresponsible proteers, they can put them to wrong use and create tremendous problems for the society. For their personal benet they present programs which are harmful to the health, morals, faith and the general economy of the society. Radio and television are very widely and intensively used these days. Most people consider them only as a source of entertainment and recreation. The children and youth are literally addicted to the idiot box.

Knowledgeable people are of opinion that the Iranian children are much more addicted to the television than the children in the developed countries like America, France, Great Britain and Japan. In Iran 40% television viewers are children, 20% youth and the rest adults. It must be remembered that the childhood and youth are the prime time for education and learning.

Whether the radio and television programs are good or bad, they will have impact on the impressionable minds of the children. Watching these programs should not be considered as harmless pastime. The child should not be given freedom to watch or listen to all the programs of his choice. Many programs will denitely be harmful to the psyche of the child.

The producers of the television and radio programs should do introspection about the damage they are causing to the delicate minds of the children by presenting shows that are very harmful for the children and youth. For them it may be the freedom of expression that drives them to their irresponsible act, but for the children and the youth, viewing these shows with keen interest, it will be sheer damnation. The parents too are responsible that they must keep a careful watch over their children's viewing of the television shows and stop them from watching bad programs.

A major part of the television programming will consist of movies and serials dealing with stories of crime, horror, murder, ghts, cheating, robbery etc. The children watch such programs with great interest. These stories can be harmful to the children in many ways. For example:

1. The impressionable and delicate minds of the children are very proactive to outside inuences. Watching such shows the children may develop restlessness, fear and horror in their minds. They may have disturbed sleep in the nights and get up shouting after

seeing bad dreams. They may start getting chronic headaches. In extreme cases, on watching the horror movies they may swoon and fall unconscious.
2. There can be very damaging effects of such movies on the morals of the children who watch them. These movies can motivate the children to commitment of crime and sins. Sometimes the children are so much impressed with the bravado of the hero of the movie that they try to emulate him in real life and land into trouble.

UNESCO has recorded in one of it's reports that 27% of youth convicted for crimes were motivated for the act after watching similar acts in the movies. In the United States of America, amongst the juvenile criminals convicted by the courts, 10% of the boys and 25% of the girls have confessed to have drawn their motivation for the crimes from the movies they had watched.[242]

According to another survey, 49% of criminals caught carrying illegal rearms, commit 28% of those who commit burglaries and 21% of acts of running away from the law derived inspiration from what they have watched in the movies. It is also reported that 25% of women who take to street walking have taken inspiration from the movies showing such stories. 54% of women have gone into houses of ill repute in emulation of famous cinema actresses.[243]

Professor Walksman of the University of Los Angeles says:

"The radiation coming out of the television screen is very harmful for the human organs. The rays coming out of the television and other household electronic appliances are of the short wave variety and the rst ill effect is that they cause headaches to those who are exposed

---

[242] Majalla Maktab Islam, v 15, Issue No.11.

[243] Majalla Maktab Islam, v 15, Issue No.11.

to them for longer spells. The thinking capacity of the person will be curbed, the blood pressure will become abnormal and the white corpuscles in the blood will be affected. These waves will have lot of impact on the nerves and cause several illnesses."[244]

Dr Alexis Carl writes:

The radio, television and inappropriate computer games destroy the emotions of the children."[245] The *Daily Ittelaat* in its Issue No.15743 reports about a European student thus:

"A college student aged 18 years was arrested and produced in the court. He is accused of kidnapping the son of a lm actor and demanding for a ransom of $ 50,000 and threatened to kill the child if the ransom money was not paid to him. In his statement to the court the accused confessed that the thought of committing the act came to his mind on watching a movie on the televisions depicting a similar act.

The police is of opinion that several such instances have come to their notice that the youths get motivated to commit crimes on watching movies on the television. A ten years old boy in Mashad, after watching a Karate show on the television, kicked his friend so hard that boy collapsed instantaneously and died.[246]

The Deputy Minister for Education and Training, Mr. Sa Niya says:

"When the television is there to effectively provide evil lessons, the best of teachers cannot do anything!"[247]

(Majalla Maktab Islam, v 18, Issue 1)

One Cuban boy, Ronny Zamora, murdered a 83 years old woman. He did this crime in Florida and is now serving a life sentence in

---

[244] Majalla Maktab Islam, v 18, Issue No.1.

[245] Majalla Maktab Islam, v 15, Issue 3

[246] Majalla Maktab Islam, v 15, Issue No.11.

[247] Majalla Maktab Islam, v 18, Issue No.1.

a prison there. His parents have sued three American television channels for damages to the tune of $2,500,000. He has produced evidence that the child had learnt about manslaughter from the television programs. Last September there was a hearing of the case in the Court when it was mentioned that when the child was small he was very fond of watching television and used to sit in front of it for eight hours at a stretch. A night before the crime, the youth watched a movie on the television where robbery at a rich woman's house was depicted.

A pretty girl of fteen years, whose name was Razaia, watched a horror movie on the television. She was so horried watching the movie that she fell down dead on the ground. When she saw in the movie that a white person was scalping the skin of the head of a black girl in the movie, she shouted in horror and had sudden cardiac arrest. The doctors said that she had a brain hemorrhage.

Dr Jalal Baremani, an expert in psychiatry says:

"The horror and adventure movies have a negative impact on the minds of the children. It is noticed that a child watching a lm depicting violent acts tried to imitate the hero and beats his brother or sister. Such movies can have a very negative effect on the future personality of the child. Watching horror movies the children become timid and cowardly. Violent movies motivate them to become violent themselves. The effects of these exposures will be there in the minds of the persons, and they might themselves get motivated to commit violent acts.

Another psychiatrist, Dr. Shukr Allah Tariqati says:

"The effects of watching bad movies on the minds of children cannot be denied. These movies have such negative effect on the children that when they grow into adults, they might themselves commit wrong acts under the inuence of the movies they had seen long ago. I therefore advise the parents not to allow their children to see such bad movies. They should take particular care to see that the children don't watch movies made and certied to be watched by adults only. They should ensure that the children don't watch any movies shown on the television after 10 PM. These are generally adult movies.".

A professor of the Tehran University, and Criminologist, Dr Ridha' Mazloomi says:

"Most of the movies shown on the television and cinema houses are harmful for our society. Their effects are so dangerous that watching a movie, a girl lost her life due to cardiac arrest seeing a horrible scene. I can put it boldly that most of the crimes and acts of terror in this world are directly related to the effects of watching movies."[248]

Dr Arnold Fremani, who works in a hospital at New York, has proved with advanced electronic gadgets that the migraine headaches and nervous weaknesses in persons are due to listening to blaring music on the FM Radio stations.[249]

The Newspaper, The Times, in one of its issues of 1964 writes:

"A pediatric doctor, made observations at two air force bases that the children of the staff in the age group of three to twelve years continuously complained of headaches, sleeplessness, insomnia and tummy troubles like diarrhoea. Medically, they were not able to establish any cause for the symptoms. After a detailed investigation it was established that the children spend long hours in front of the television screens. The doctors recommended that the children should be stopped from watching the television. This regime was effective that the complaints like headaches, nausea, vomiting and diarrhoea in the children had tapered off.[250]

The thoughtful parents who love their children should not allow

---

[248] Daily Ittelaat, 10 Aban, 1352

[249] Majalla Maktab Islam, v 15, Issue 3

[250] Paiwandhai Kudak wa Khanwada, p. 131

them to watch television for long hours, particularly in the nights. They should allow them to watch only such programs that are not harmful to their spirit and mind.

The Gender Problems

Sexuality is one of the most sensitive instincts of the human nature. This in fact is a highly constructive instinct of the human race. It will have both positive and negative effects on the psychological and physiological life of the human beings. Many acts of the human beings and the causes of several physical and psychological ailments can be attributed to this instinct.

If the upbringing of the individual takes place in a proper and thoughtful manner, the instinct of sex can prove a boon for the welfare and contentment of the person. But if the upbringing is in an atmosphere of lechery, lasciviousness and excesses, there is every probability that the instinct of sexuality might become the cause of many physical and psychological aberrations that can become denite cause of ultimate destruction of the person in this life and Hereafter.

It is not proper to think that the instinct of sexuality manifests itself only after puberty. The instinct will be present in every individual since birth; however, it remains dormant for quite some time. Even then, it manifests itself at different times during the childhood in a subtle way. Sometimes small children fondle their genitals and feel pleasure. This creates in them a sort of emotion.

They feel the pleasure when the parents caress and kiss them. They feel attracted towards beautiful persons and things, and sometimes they express these feelings in words too. At the age of two or three years the children start distinguishing between boys and girls and look at one another's private parts with deep interest. When they grow up a little, they are attracted to beautiful pictures. They look at them with surprise. Sometimes they might utter bad words. They start showing inclination towards the opposite sex. They try to have the attention of the persons of the opposite gender.

Sometimes, they even ask the parents questions concerning sex. They try to eavesdrop over the whisperings of the parents. They like to sit with friends in a quiet corner and exchange secrets. All these go to prove that the children have within them the latent instinct of sex that tries to nd expression in their actions. Without proper guidance and knowledge, the instinct keeps driving the children. They won't know what they want. Their only attention is to derive pleasure from any source. But they don't know how to get this pleasure. Till the age of ten to twelve years the children continue in this state of suspense. From the age of twelve to fteen, the instinct of sexuality dawns on them with speed.

Responsible parents will not be oblivious of this instinct of their children. They cannot continue without devising a strategy to properly handle the matter. Sex education is one of the most difcult and delicate aspects of the education of children. Slightest mistake or neglect on the part of the parents might push the children into the abyss of destruction.

The parents should focus their attention towards the fact that prior to puberty the children won't have the faculty of procreation. Therefore God has kept the instinct of sex latent in them. It is in the best interest of the children that their instinct of sexuality does not have a premature awakening. If this happens prematurely, the child will suffer many types of social stigmas and physical ailments.

The parents must abstain from everything that might provoke the sex instinct in the children. They must provide to them such healthy environment that their minds don't get diverted towards premature expression of sex instinct. The thoughtful parents can themselves decide what is desirable for the children and what is not. But here we are mentioning a few of the things that the parents would like to keep in their minds.

They should discreetly ensure that the children don't touch their private parts, they don't look at pictures of models in the magazines, listen to love ditties and watch romantic movies, praise good looks and beauty of others, stare at beautiful faces and exposed limbs of others, intently listen to bawdy jokes or courtship of the parents or other elders. These and many other attractions might cause a utter in the sex instinct of the child.

The parents should not allow children of ve to six years of age to live unattended. They might sometimes play with each other's private parts and emotions might awaken in them. The children should not be allowed to lie in their beds when they are awake. Have separate beds for children of the age of six years.

If the children sleep on the same bed, their bodies might rub against each other and give rise to the sex instinct. The parents should not make children of ve to six years of age sleep with them in the same bed. This should be particularly so in the case of a child of the opposite sex. Even the mother should not rub her body with the body of her six –year-old daughter.

The Prophet of Islam has said:

"When the child reaches the age of seven years, arrange a separate bed for him."[251] Imam as-Sadiq narrates from his ancestors:

---

[251] Makarim al akhlaq, v 1, 256

"The women and children of ten years must have separate individual beds."[252]

"If a mother rubs her body against the body of her own daughter, she is doing a sort of molestation."[253]

"A man should not kiss his six year old daughter, and a woman should not kiss her seven year old son."[254]

It is a practice in many households that the women move around in partially revealing dresses. Many men too are not far behind in this. They will have loincloth up to their knees and keep moving around in the house with the sons and daughters present. They think that they are all members of the same family and Mahram, or close relations, from whom the women don't have to hide.

The parents also think that their exposed limbs will not affect their children and that they are still very young to be conscious of any such thing. They think that their daughters' breasts not covered with a cloth (chador) and exposed limbs will not affect their son in any way. This they think because the children are brother and sister to one another. This is not the right thinking. The instinct of sex is one of the strongest instincts and when aroused it may not allow the person to think of any relationship.

Imam 'Ali, The Commander of the Faithful, says:

"It is very much possible that at a glimpse the instinct of love and sex might awaken."[255]

Such mercurial urges might become the cause of grave consequence to the innocent children. Perhaps in such circumstances the child might commit rape or incest. For any such thing the parents will be

---

[252] Wasail al shiah, v 14, p. 268

[253] Wasail al shiah, v 14, p. 170

[254] Wasail al shiah, v 14, p. 170

[255] Gharar al hukm, p. 416

squarely responsible for their careless attitude.

Here it will be in place to quote the writing of an intellectual:

"For the psychic welfare of the children, we should not expose our bodies to them. Sometimes the children might peep through the crevices in the bathroom door while we are bathing. or changing our clothes. We must ensure that the children don't develop such habits."[256]

This is true that the parents are Mahram for their children and can live in the same house together. But the parents should not sacrice the collective rights of the children for their pleasure and freedom. This way they would be exposing their children to ruination. As a consequence their lives will be condemned to shame and melancholy.

A person's thigh was exposed from his robe. The Prophet noticed this and said.: "Hide your thigh, because it is one of the things that shall not be exposed to others."[257]

It is not proper that a four years old son takes a shower along with his mother. Similarly a four years old daughter should not bathe with her father. The children and youth should not remain alone doing nothing. Loneliness might create the urge for masturbation. The private parts of a small boy must be kept covered, not exposed, to his other siblings. Never use abusive invectives with the children. The husband and wife should not sleep on one bed in the presence of their children. They should not play pranks on each other while the children are around.

One problem of a couple with children is the sexual relations between the man and wife. It is a right of the couple to sleep together. But when there are a few children in the family, there will be the problem of having some privacy. Any way, they should

---

[256] Paiwand hai Kudak wa Khanwada, p. 177

[257] Mustadrak al-wasail, Hakim, v 4, p. 181.

continue their private relationship without giving a hint about it to the children. Otherwise there will be the danger of the sexual urge rising in the children and, at their age, it would be prone with horrible consequences.

Imam Ja'far as-Sadiq says:

"The husband should not go near his wife while the child is in their bed room. Otherwise it will be like committing a rape."[258]

The Prophet of Islam has said:

"By Allah! someone copulates with his wife when his child is in the room, and the child looks at them and hears their sound, then that child will never prosper. Be it a girl or a boy, either will get besmirched in adultery (for the mere observation of the act)."

Whenever Imam Zain ul Abidin wanted to be near his spouse, he used to send out his servants, bolt the door from inside and put down the curtains.[259]

The Prophet of Islam has prohibited man coming near his wife when the little baby looks at them from the cradle.[260]

Therefore the husband and wife who have a child, should not be as unrestricted as they used to be before getting the child. To guard the chastity of the children, the couple should keep their conjugal life totally away from their view. This may not be so easy a process. But they have no other alternative.

They should not think that the child is innocent and will not comprehend anything at that age. But to the contrary, the children are very sharp. They will deduce their own conclusions from what they observe. They will be inquisitive to know what the parents do in privacy.

---

[258] Wasail al shiah, v 14, p. 94

[259] Wasail al shiah, v 14, p. 94

[260] Mustadrak al-wasail, v 2, p. 546

Sometimes even they pretend to be asleep to know and see what is going on. They also try to peep from behind the doors and curtains. It is better if the parents have a secure, private room for themselves in the house. As far as possible this room should be at some distance from the children's quarters. The children should be trained to announce their arrival when they enter the parents' room. The parents should avoid their conjugal affairs when the children are around at home, or until they have not soundly gone to sleep.

A Western intellectual writes thus:

"Most modern dwellings are made in such a way that the planners overlook the privacy for the conjugal relations of the inmates. In fact the homes these days can be termed as the dwellings that are against sexual requirements of the dwellers. Most homes or apartments are such that there is no provision of separate bedroom for the parents. And if they are there, the walls of the rooms are so thin that the children living in the next room can hear even if the children whisper sweet nothings to each other. .It is a bitter fact that because of not having a proper place for their conjugal life, the parents will have a suffocated existence."[261]

But one disadvantage of the parents sleeping in a separate bedroom is that they will not know what the children are up to. Particularly when there is a slightly grown up boy and there is also a girl in the group of the children. In this situation leaving the children together in one room may not be advisable. In a situation of this type, the parents may have to sacrice their own convenience. If the parents have to sleep with the children in the same dormitory, they should use separate beds. For their conjugal satisfaction they shall have to nd a quiet corner late in the night when all the kids have gone to sleep. When the parents are responsible persons and they have the will, they

---

[261] Paiwand hai Kudak wa Khanwada, p. 176

can nd solution to the problem without much difculty.

Allah says in The Holy Qur'an:

> "O ye who believe Let those whom your right hands possess and those of you who have not reached puberty seek permission of you three times (a day) (ere they come into your presence) before the morning prayer, and when ye lay aside your garments for the heat (at midday), These are the three times of privacy for you; It is neither for you nor for them a sin (if) after those (three times) ; some of you go round attending upon the others; Thus doth God maketh clear unto you the signs; and God is all-Knowing, All-Wise."
> (The Holy Qur'an, 24:58)

Before puberty the children ask direct and indirect questions about sex. Some parents avoid such questions. For example they say:, 'Keep quiet Don't ask such silly questions!' 'These things don't concern you!' 'You will understand everything when you grow up!'

They can momentarily quieten the children with these vague replies. But some parents do give replies to the child's questions. But these answers too are wrong and contrary to the facts. The child subtly understands that the parents are not telling the truth to him.

Both the above attitudes are wrong. Because the child is asking questions out of his thirst for knowledge, and if he is not given a proper reply, he might be more inquisitive and might get information from other quarters that may not be in his best interests.

Fortunately, the questions asked by the children about sex prior to puberty are not so complicated that answering them could be very difcult for the parents. The one question that troubles every child is the difference between the private parts of a boy and a girl. A child fully understands that there is difference between his private part and that of his sister. But he wants to know, why this difference?.

Sometimes he fears that he has some defect in himself that he is not like his sister. At other times he thinks that the sister is defective. He wants to know the cause for the difference and asks for an explanation from the parents. It is the duty of the parents to give a satisfactory reply to the child. They must tell him that all boys are made like him and all the girls are like his sister. Then the boys grow up to be fathers and the girls grow into mothers. They will have the children of their own and the cycle will thus go on and on.

You need not imagine for a moment that the child wants to know all the facts about sex in one go. He wants to get the answer only for what he has in his mind at that moment. Neither anything more, nor less than it Before a child reaches the age of understanding, he must be informed about sex to the extent it is absolutely necessary and within his easy comprehension.

If you don't reply to his queries, he might pick up harmful details from the elder urchins in the neighborhood or from the other boys at school. If you guide the child properly, he will be safe from damaging information from other quarters.

When your child attains puberty, and you know that his sexual instinct has awakened to an extent, and there is speedy metamorphosis in him, then at an appropriate moment you must inform him thus:

When children grow up, they will have a desire to have a companion. The girls like boys as companions and the boys like the girls. There is no harm in this. But, if the companion is pious and gentle, then it will be fortunate for both the boy and the girl. Otherwise, a bad companion for a person can be a curse for him or her.

After marriage the responsibilities multiply many times. The expenses on the wife and, when the children arrive, the expenses keep mounting. All these responsibilities have to be borne by the husband. You too must complete your education properly that you settle into a good job. Then we can arrange your marriage. Work hard at your studies. If you are a capable person, people will like you and you can get a good bride for yourself.

Beware of masturbation. It is a sin. It is also harmful for a person's health. A person who does it, may not be suitable marriage later on.

Avoid bad company and don't pick the habits of bad friends. Some of these habits destroy a person."

When children grow, they start getting furze in their armpits and the pubic area. The children get scared seeing this for the rst time. Guide them appropriately. Explain to them the method of removing the unnecessary hairs. The girl starts getting menses. When she sees the blood stains on her clothing, she gets scared. Guide her about the periodic menstruation that a girl gets after puberty. Her breasts start growing, some girls get worried about this development too.

Similarly when the son shows the signs of puberty, he will see disturbing dreams in his sleep. During the dreams his emotions will rise and ejaculation will come. Sometimes, innocent and ignorant, children think that they have some serious disease. Sometimes they think that they are committing a sin. They worry and keep the matter to themselves as a closely guarded secret. In such times, it is the duty of the parents to prepare the child in advance.

The mother should take the daughter into condence and explain to her that getting hair in certain regions of the body and bleeding periods with the onset of puberty are normal phenomena for girls. She must teach the daughter about the personal hygiene during these periods and the method of cleansing after the period is over. She must also be told that during the periods she should not observe fasts nor should she offer her mandatory prayers. The *Ramadhan* fasts that she has missed during the period, she can observe later on, at her convenience.

The father too should tell to his son that he is a grown up person now. He will get hair in his arm-pits and the pubic region. He will experience emotional dreams with ejaculation. This is a normal phenomenon with all boys who have attained puberty. He needn't worry about this. Whenever he ejaculated in his dream, he will have to take the mandatory cleansing bath. The father should explain to the son the method of taking the cleansing bath. In this way the parents can put the minds of their children, who are at the threshold of adult life now, at rest.

The Habit of Reading Books

Books are one of the best tools for training and upbringing. A good book always has a salutary effect on the mind of a reader. It will elevate spirit and thoughts. It will augment his store of knowledge. Books help in correcting moral ineptitude.

Particularly in these days of mechanical existence, when people have hardly any time to attend meetings and symposia, the best source of acquiring religious and general knowledge are books that can be browsed whenever a person nds some time to spare. It is possible that the reading of book might have a deeper impact on the minds of the readers than the other sources of acquiring knowledge.

Sometimes, reading brings about a revolutionary change in the outlook of a person. The habit of reading is the best pastime. It can keep a person busy when he has nothing else to do. The persons who are in the habit of reading, not only make the best use of their spare time but they will keep their minds away from the worries that might chase them if they sit brooding, doing nothing. A good book, for a reader, is better than visiting the best of gardens and scenic places.

'Ali, The Commander of the Faithful, says:

"A person who keeps himself occupied with books, will never lose his peace of mind."[262]

"Obtaining fresh knowledge remove the tiredness and cloudiness of your hearts; because the hearts, like the bodies, too experience exhaustion."[263]

The gauge for the progress and civilization of any nation is the quality and the number of books and the number of persons habituated of reading them. Formal education of a person is no criterion of judging a person's learning. A really learned person is one who is engaged in meaningful reading and research. We unfortunately have lots of persons with school diplomas and university degrees but very few learned scholars and researchers. Most children, when they complete their formal education, keep aside the books and get busy with other activities of life.

The growth of knowledge of these persons gets stagnant from that time. Their criterion of acquiring education for nding a job has been achieved. They feel that there is no further use for any more knowledge. In fact, education should be for achieving excellence in the chosen eld of knowledge. Education is a continuous process and goes on till the last breath of a person. The Religion of Islam too has exhorted its followers to pursue the path of learning from the cradle to the grave.

The Prophet of Islam has said:

"Search for knowledge is the duty of every Muslim. Allah likes the seekers of knowledge."[264] Imam Ja'far as-Sadiq says:

"Even if my companions are motivated to acquire knowledge at the threat of a whipping, I would approve of it."[265]

---

[262] Gharar al hukm, p. 636

[263] Usul al-Ka, v 1, p. 48

[264] Usul al-Ka, Vol1, p. 30

[265] Usul al-Ka, v 1, p. 33

The Prophet of Islam has said:

"Barring two types of persons, there is no reward for anyone else; First the erudite scholar and then he who is busy acquiring knowledge."[266]

Imam Ja'far as-Sadiq said:

"Persons are of three types: 1. The erudite scholar, 2. The seeker of knowledge, and 3. The others are mere a heap of garbage."[267]

Luqman, the Prophet, told to his son, ' Spare some time in the day and night for reading and acquiring knowledge. If you stop reading, your knowledge will dissipate.'[268]

Imam Ja'far as-Sadiq said:

"Search for knowledge in all conditions is absolutely necessary."[269]

The Prophet of Islam has said:

"Search for knowledge is the duty of every Muslim man and every Muslim woman."[270] Imam Ja'far as-Sadiq says:

"If the people knew the uses of knowledge, they would have tried to acquire it even at the cost of their very lives. For this purpose they would have undertaken hazardous sea voyages."[271]

The Prophet has said:

"If I spent one day without adding to the store of my knowledge, I would consider that day unlucky for me."[272]

It is the duty of the parents to send their children to schools for acquiring knowledge of reading and writing. Islam has very clear

---

[266] Usul al-Ka, v 1, p. 33

[267] Usul al-Ka, v 1, p. 34

[268] Bihar al-anwar, v 1, p. 169

[269] Bihar al-anwar, v 1, p. 172

[270] Bihar al-anwar, v 1, p. 177

[271] Bihar al-anwar, v 1, p. 177

[272] Majma al zawaid, v 1, p. 127

directions in this regard for the followers of the faith:

Imam Ja'far as-Sadiq says:

"A child plays for seven years, studies for seven years and for another seven years learns about what is permissible (*halal*) and im-permissible (*haram*)."[273]

The Prophet of Islam has said: "A son has three rights over his father: 1. The father must select a good name for him. 2. The father should teach him to read and write, and 3. when he grows up, get him a spouse."[274]

"When a child is taken to the school, and the teacher instructs him to say Bism Allah (In the name of Allah Almighty), Allah will spare the child's parents from the re of the Hell!"[275]

"Pity on the children of the Last Epoch, for what their forebears have brought to them. Although the parents would themselves be Muslims, they would not acquaint the children with the religious duties."[276]

The other responsibility of the parents is that they bring up their children in such a way they cultivate the habits of reading good books and become researchers of knowledge. The atmosphere in their homes should be one of education and learning. They must motivate the children by their words and actions to cultivate the habit of reading.

Before the child goes for formal education to the school, he should be introduced to books. In the beginning the parents must read out books to the child. They should read small and interesting stories and fables to make the child interested in books. Give the children books with lots of multicolor pictures and illustrations.

Every day, the parents or the elder siblings should read to the child

---

[273] Mustadrak al-wasail, v 2, p. 624

[274] Mustadrak al-wasail, v 2, p. 625

[275] Mustadrak al-wasail, v 2, p. 625

[276] Mustadrak al-wasail, v 2, p. 625

a part of the book to keep his sustained interest in the contents. They should explain to the child about the illustrations in the book. Then the child should be asked to recount the story and tell about the illustration printed with the story. In this informal education, the parents should not make haste in teaching and should not give to him any books that are beyond his comprehension. They must rst make the child interested in listening to stories, then bring the process of reading out from the books.

Continue this process till the child learns to read and write himself. Then leave the work of reading the books to the child. Sometimes ask the opinion of the child about a new book that he has read. Discuss the contents of the book with him. .Continue giving attention till the child becomes habituated of reading books.

Here the parents must be reminded of certain points:

1. The children like stories and fables and understand their contents well. It is therefore useful the material provided to them on any subject should be in the form of stories.
2. Every child will have his own individual personality. The capability and tastes too will differ from person to person. There will be changes in the tastes of a person with advancements in years. Therefore, the parents must rst try to gauge the taste and the capability of their child and then bring the books to suit his requirements. Don't thrust difcult and boring contents on the child. This might have negative impact on the child's reading habit.
3. Since the child is in the process of developing his personality, and the books can have deep impact on this process, care must be exercised to see that books with appropriate content are chosen for him. The parents should rst read the books themselves, then decide about their suitability for the child's reading. The child

should not read any undesirable matter that might have negative impact on his impressionable mind. If he gets into the habit of reading such literature, it might be difcult to wean him out of it.

4. Children show more interest in reading about crime and adventure. These books may have deleterious effect on the psyche of the child. Similarly books that give vent to the sexual instincts in the child should be kept out of his reach.

One person writes in his memoirs thus: ' My Granny used to love me very much. I used to sleep with her in the nights. I always used to ask her to tell me bed-time-stories. To make me go to sleep, she used to tell me one story every night. In her repertoire there were stories about the Jinn Baba and other tales of horror.

These stories have left their mark on my psyche. I used to sleep in the feeling of horror after hearing the stories. I started seeing horrible bad dreams. Over time, I turned into a timid and cowardly person. I was always afraid to be alone. I became excitable and restless. This condition persists with me. How I wish parents and elders don't relate horror stories to their impressionable children. I have decided that I will not tell such stories to my own children. I generally tell them stories from the Holy The Holy Qur'an and other stories with good morals.'

1. The habit of reading is not just a pastime. The main purpose of reading is to acquire knowledge and understand the contents of the books and deriving advantage from them. It is not very important how many books the child reads, but the important thing is how he has read them. Is he just making a cursory rapid reading? Has he read a book with absorbed interest and understood its contents? The parents should give full attention to this aspect. Occasionally, they must ask the child to give the

gist of a book he has read. They should derive their conclusion if the child has understood the contents correctly or not. They should correct the child, if his understanding of the contents is not correct.

2. Children generally like books with imaginary stories. Some intellectuals encourage reading of such books. They feel that such book will encourage the imaginative faculties of the child. But the author feels that the reading of imaginary and ctitious stories can promote the habit of lying in the child. His mind will become the storehouse of false thoughts. When he grows up, he might allude to falsehoods to fulll his needs and wishes.

3. It is true that a child prefers to read stories than other reading matter. But care must be taken that he is given a carefully selected mix of books on various subjects and not just the story-books. The child must slowly develop interest in reading and understanding intricate subject matter of serious literature.

4. It is not true that the children are fond of only ctitious stories. They will denitely show keen interest in reading the stories of great personalities, their lives and achievements. They can have their role models in these personages and aim to model their own lives on the lives of the great personages.

Physically Handicapped Children

Some children are physically handicapped from birth, others develop inrmities after accidents. There are many physical disabilities like blindness, lameness, deafness, dumbness etc. There are other children, who may not have any physical abnormalities, but they might be abnormally short, fat, with jutting teeth, small and sunken eyes and several such features.

There is no fault of the individuals with these aberrations. Allah has given birth to them, as they are. All the creations have their own beauty, it is our thinking that makes yardsticks for judging good looks.

Since the disabled individuals will be conscious of their disability, they will be sad and subject to the feeling of inferiority. If efforts are not made to remove this feeling from their minds, they will always be sad and morose.

With the inferiority complex in him, a person loses his vibrant personality. They start thinking that they are incapable of any good. They will be reluctant to accept responsibilities and come forward to work with alacrity. They literally surrender ignominiously. They might even have access to criminal thoughts as a rebellion against their pitiable condition in the social fabric.

Physically Handicapped Children

The disabled are pitiable. It is the duty of the other members of the society to put such handicapped persons at ease. They should give them the same treatment as they give to any normal person. They should not make them conscious of their defect through any overt or covert act. Some people cut practical jokes on the handicapped persons making their defect a matter of ridicule. This will be like piercing their hearts with arrows.

Islam strictly prohibits laughing about the physical defects of others. This attitude is counted amongst the major sins a person can commit. There is order for so much care in this matter that the believers are required not even to do anything that can slightly remind the handicapped person of his defect.

The Prophet of Islam has said:

"Don't stare at people under distress and at the lepers, lest your looks provoke the feelings of sadness and shame in their hearts."[277]

It is the responsibility of Muslims to show more attention and care to such persons with a view to ameliorate their feelings of sadness. They must encourage the handicapped to lead as normal a life as possible. The parents of handicapped children carry an onerous responsibility. They should remember that even the handicapped are having the capacity to excel. If the parents try to fathom the aptitude of such children and help them to utilize their latent capabilities properly, they can be molded into efcient and skilled persons. They can excel in scientic and technical elds.

Thus they can achieve respected positions in the society. There are innumerable instances of handicapped persons scaling big heights in different activities and reaching the pinnacle of success despite their defects. The parents should not be conscious of their child's defects and also abstain. from mentioning about it to anyone, at least not in

---

[277] Bihar al-anwar, v 75, p. 15

the presence of the child himself or his siblings.

They should not mention about the defect in the child even in a commiserating manner. Their treatment of this child should not be any different than the treatment they give to their other normal children. If a handicapped child expresses his anxiety about his defect, the parents must try to put him at ease.

Remind him of, and praise, his other faculties and encourage him to make good use of them to prove himself a useful member of the society.

The parents must make a careful study of the latent capabilities in the handicapped child and then consult knowledgeable persons to seek their advice and recommendations for the right course of action. Then they should humor and encourage the child to try and develop the chosen skills. The parents will thus be doing a great service to the society by making their handicapped child a useful member of the community.

Thus, the handicapped person would, in a way, overcome his handicap and make the best use of the talent gifted by Allah to him.

A girl writes in her letter thus:

"A friend of mine told her life's story to me in these words:

'One day I fell down to the ground from the terrace when I was thirteen years old. My back-bone was fractured which rendered me a handicapped person for life. For some time I got treatment at a hospital. Although I had terric pain, later on I realized that the days at the hospital were the better days for me than what I suffered after returning home.

When I was discharged from the hospital and reached home, my parents started treating me as a sworn enemy. They used to say, 'You are the cause of shame and ill luck for us How can we tell others that we are the parents of a crippled daughter? You will remain foisted on us forever Instead of consoling me for my predicament, day and night they were taunting me.

They never for a moment thought that I was the victim of an unfortunate accident and personally not responsible for what happened. to me. I used to plead to Allah every day to give me death and release me from the life I was living With my paralyzed legs, I used to drag myself around the house and do the work. None ever bothered about my predicament. In fact my parents stopped considering me their daughter.

My youth was being spent in sorrow and pain. At the age of 15 I looked like an old woman of fty. My parents died and my brothers and sisters never bothered about me. After sometime I was married. My husband was a very kind person. He loved me very much. Prior to this I had forgotten what is love and affection. Now my condition started to improve day by day. I am now a hale and hearty person. Allah has given me children. I am now spending a happy and contented life.'"

Physical Punishment

Lots of parents give physical punishment to their children in the interest of proper upbringing. Even some teachers too contribute to this attitude. They believe that the devils cannot be tamed with mere words. In the past a majority of people believed in this dictum. Those days the canes, chains and whips were considered important tools to be handy with a school.

The parents desirous of good upbringing of their children never abstained from beating them when required. But most intellectuals consider this tyrannical method of upbringing as barbaric and harmful for the children. In most developed countries of the world there is almost a total ban on the physical punishment for correction of children.

A child cannot be reformed through physical punishments. Perhaps, it might have a temporary effect on the child, but will be very harmful in a longer run. For example:

1. When a child is beaten, he gets habituated of bowing down his head to torture and force. He may perhaps start thinking that force is the only key to success. He starts thinking that when

one is angry, he should beat. By giving physical punishment to the children, the parents set an example for them to adopt the tyrannical laws of the jungle in their future lives.
2. The children who get beatings, develop hate and antagonism against their parents. The children never forget the harsh treatment they received at the hands of the parents. Such children might even become rebellious.
3. Repeated beatings can make a child timid and cowardly. The personality of the child can also be suppressed with physical punishment. He might later on become a victim of psychological ailments.
4. In most cases physical punishment seldom improves the child. It doesn't create a wish in the child to correct his behavior. He might perhaps show some momentary signs of change out of fear of the rod and the beatings, but is no guarantee that he will not repeat the same act again. His basic failing will persist in his subconscious mind. It will manifest itself later on in some other form.

One person says:

"My twelve year old son picked up some money from my wife's wardrobe. When I came to know about this, I punished him with a stick. From that time, he never went near his mother's wardrobe.

It is true that the boy did not pick anything else from his mother's wardrobe. The father appears to have succeeded by meting out physical punishment to the child. But the matter was not so simple.

The story proceeded further. The boy found other subterfuges to continue his bad activities. He started boarding the omnibus and avoiding to pay the fare to the conductor. When his mother asked him to shop at the grocers, he would pinch the change. Later on it was learned that he has stolen money from his friends too. The conclusion of the story is that, when the child was beaten for one fault, he cleverly didn't repeat that act. But his mind worked overtime, and he invented other methods of committing thefts.[278]

One intellectual writes:

"The children who receive corrective beatings, become weak and useless persons. Or, otherwise they turn into stubborn and deceitful persons. They seem to be taking revenge of the ill treatment received in their childhood."[279]

Mr Russel writes:

"In my opinion, physical punishment of children is not right in any way."[280] Islam too has termed physical punishment harmful and has prohibited it. 'Ali, The Commander of the Faithful, says:

"The intelligent person gets guidance through politeness, it is only the animals that cannot be corrected without beatings."[281]

Imam Ja'far as-Sadiq says:

"Whoever whips another person once, Allah will shower the ery whip against him."[282] The Prophet of Islam said:

"Use love and affection in education and upbringing and don't have access to cruelty because a wise mentor is better than a cruel one."[283]

One person said that he complained about his son to Imam Moosa bin Ja'far. The Imam replied, "Don't ever beat him But maintain a distance from him, and this distance too should not be kept for too long!"[284]

---

[278] Ruwan Shinasi Tajrubi Kudak, p. 263

[279] Ruwan Shinashi Tajrubi Kudak, p. 266

[280] Dar Tarbiat, p. 169

[281] Gharar al hukm, p. 236

[282] Wasail al shiah, v 19, p. 14

[283] Bihar al-anwar, v 77, p. 175

[284] Bihar al-anwar, v104, p. 99

Physical Punishment

Physical punishments are very harmful for the upbringing of the children and they must be avoided. But if there is no other way of correcting the child, adopt it as a last resort. Islam too permits this in certain conditions.

The Prophet of Islam has said:

"Ask your children to start offering prayers at the age of six years. If they don't listen to your repeated warnings, you may beat them to become regular at offering prayers when they are seven years old."[285]

In another tradition Imam Ja'far as-Sadiq says:

"When the child is nine years old, teach him to do the Wudhu' (the ablution prior to offering prayers); order him to do the Wudhu' and pray. If the child doesn't obey, beat him and make him offer prayers."[286]

Imam 'Ali has said:

"As you reprimand your own son, so can you reprimand an orphan. And the occasion on which you might beat your son, you can beat the orphan on a similar occasion."[287]

"If your slave disobeys Allah, beat him. If he disobeys you, forgive him."[288]

One person came to the presence of the Prophet of Islam and said that an orphaned child was in his care. He wanted to know if he can beat the child to correct him. The Prophet replied:

"In a situation where you can beat your son, you may beat the orphan on a similar situation in his best interests."[289]

It is always better not to make access to the physical punishment of

---

[285] Mustadrak al-wasail, v 1, p. 171

[286] Wasail al shiah, v 3, p. 13

[287] Wasail al shiah, v 15, p. 197

[288] Gharar al hukm, p. 115

[289] Mustadrak al-wasail, v 2, p. 625

children as far as possible. And when it becomes necessary, make use of maximum restraint in the matter. The punishment must be well thought out and appropriate to the occasion.

One person asked the Prophet of Islam:

"The members of my family don't obey me. How should I reform them ?" The Prophet replied: "Forgive them!." The man repeated the question a second, and a third time. The Holy Prophet gave the same reply; but then he said: "If you wish to reprimand your people, then you must keep in mind that the punishment should not be more than their misdemeanor. You should also abstain from beating them on their faces."[290]

Imam Ja'far as-Sadiq has said:

"If needed, don't inict more than ve or six blows to your child or the servant and these blows should not be too severe."[291]

While reprimanding children, better don't do it in the presence of others. Others' presence might cause mental torture to the children and might harm them. If the beating is excessive, there is a Deet or ne prescribed in Islam for one who inicts the punishment. Therefore, care must be exercised while beating the children to correct them. According to the Islamic Laws, if a person's face turns black on account of the beating, the ne is six Gold Dinars (coins). If the face turns blue, three dinars and for a red face, a Dinar and Half.[292]

The parents have no right to behave like tyrants with their children. They must not kick them, box them and beat them with chains and rods.

Islam does permit reprimanding and beating the child for purposes of correction and, in fact, orders such action. We nd that the youth in

---

[290] Majma al zawaid, v 8, p. 106

[291] Wasail al shiah, v 18, p. 581

[292] Wasail al shiah, v 19, p. 295

the Western countries go astray because of excess of freedom given to them.

Non-Physical Punishment

Lots of parents prefer to give non-physical punishments to their children in times of need. For example, if a child misbehaves, he is locked in a dark room or a big trunk. Sometimes the parents shout and use bad language in anger when a child commits a mistake. The impact of such cruel punishments may not be far less than the physical punishments discussed in the previous chapter.

Imam 'Ali, The Commander of the Faithful, says:

"There are many types of punishments which have bigger impact than physical assault."[293]

It is possible that these punishments might be more severe on the minds of the children than the physical punishments. These punishments will injure the personality of the child and create elements of fear and restlessness in his nature. It has happened many a time that when a child is locked alone in a dark room, the effect on his nerves was so severe that he was not able to erase it from his mind for a major part of his life.

Some of the victims of such nervousness sometimes swoon under

---

[293] Gharar al hukm, p. 415

its effect. The parents should therefore refrain from giving such punishments to the children. Shouting and using foul language with the children is taboo (*haram*) and will have a very damaging impact on their upbringing. This might motivate the children to learn such foul language for their future lives.

But denitely there are several non-physical punishments that will not have any negative impact on the minds of the children, and at the same time they are very effective in correcting them. For example, if a child misbehaves or doesn't give proper attention to his studies, the parents stop speaking with him for a time or don't take him out on picnics.

Sometimes, as a punishment the parents don't take a child out to a party where the family is invited. Sometimes, as a reprimand, a child is made to miss a meal. At other time, as a corrective, the child is given some difcult task to do. These punishments, used judiciously, might be very effective in controlling and correcting the child. They will not be accompanied with any deleterious effect on the mind and the nerves of the child.

But punishments are punishments. There is one denite defect in punishments that they are not much effective for correcting the intrinsic defects in the nature of a child. With the fear of punishment the child might momentarily, or for some time, behave differently and properly. Or he might cleverly not make the same mistake openly. But when he nds a suitable opportunity, he might be up to the same behavior for which he has been reprimanded in the past.

The punishments, therefore, don't cut away the cause of the misdemeanors of the child. It is possible that sometimes the child might take shelter behind lying and stealth. To make effective and judicious of the non-physical punishments, a few points are suggested to the parents and the mentors of the children:

1. The punishment should be well thought out and commensurate with the misdemeanor of the child. Ensure that the punishment is not more than the aw or the misbehavior of the child. If the child thinks that the punishment was unjust, he might react in his defense and start to be rebellious and head-strong.
2. The punishment should not be such that the child starts thinking that the parents are his enemies and they don't love him.
3. If the child has committed something wrong unintentionally, he should not be punished. Despite this, if the child is punished, it might have negative impact on his feelings and his mind.
4. Punishments should not become an every day affair if the parents wish them to be effective. If punishments are repeated too often, the child might turn into a compulsive offender. Then the punishments will not have any effect on him.
5. Imam 'Ali has said: "Reprimand and punishment in excess might make one stubborn."[294]
6. The child can be punished for a single act and not on a collective basis for his past Misbehaviors. Otherwise the child will be confused as to why he is being punished. He will not repeat an act, only if he knows that he was punished for doing that. It is always better that the punishment is immediately after the commitment of the act.
7. To the extent possible, efforts must be made to see that the punishment is according to the mistake he has committed. For example, if the child has fallen behind in doing the exercises of mathematics, he must be ordered to complete the exercise and not to copy the entire book of mathematics from start to end. If the child has carelessly thrown away his school bag, and the uniform, after returning from school, he must be asked to

---

[294] Gharar al hukm, p. 70

immediately arrange them properly in the right place.

8. As a punishment for this careless behavior he should not be threatened that he would not be taken to the dinner scheduled for that evening. If the child had misbehaved at a party, his punishment can be not taking out to the next party and not stopping his allowance of the pocket money. If the child squanders his pocket money, then, as a punishment a similar amount may be cut from his next allowance.

9. After the punishment, the parents should not mention his mistake again and again. One person says that he complained about his son to Moosa bin Ja'far. He replied, "Don't beat him. Just be cross with him But this attitude of yours should not be for long."[295]

10. If you wish to punish a child, don't compare him with other children. Don't recount the qualities of the other children to him. You cannot reform the child through this attitude. You might give rise to the feeling of jealousy in the mind of the child.

One person writes in his memoirs thus:

"In my childhood my father used to shout at me very much. He used to insult me in the presence of relatives and my friends. He always recounted others achievements in front of me. He always looked for an occasion to belittle me. He considered me an inferior person. However much he insulted me, I became more stubborn. I lost interest in my studies. I had developed an inferiority complex. I started shirking work. I was not willing to accept any responsibility. My personality was injured because of constant nagging by my father. Today I am a lazy and lonely person."

---

[295] Gharar al hukm, p. 70

Encouragement and Reward

One very good method of good upbringing is the appreciation and encouragement when a child performs well. This will have a salutary effect on the mind of the child. It will provide him the reason to do still better in the future. Every human being loves himself. In his own way he thinks of developing and advancing his personality. He wants that others recognize and appreciate his personality. If he receives the appreciation of others, he will strive for further improvement. But if he is discouraged, his enthusiasm will be dampened. A few suggestions for obtaining good results are given here:

1. The actions of the child can be appreciated, but not too often. Because , if the appreciation is too much, it might lose its importance in the eyes of the child. He may then take your appreciation as a matter of routine.
2. The appreciation of the child should be at a specic place and time so that he realizes why and for what he is being commended. Then he will try to perform better and earn appreciation on other occasions too. This is the reason that repeated and unnecessary

appreciation is not advisable. For example, if a child is repeatedly given a pat on his back that he is a good and polite individual, it might lose its signicance for him. The child will not be able to comprehend the reason for the appreciation.
3. It is also necessary that good acts and works of the child are appreciated and not his person. This way he will understand that he is praised for what he does, and not for what he is the importance of every person is because of his achievements.
4. While praising a child, never compare him with other children. For example the father should not tell to his son, "You are a good and truthful boy, unlike Hasan who is a liar."This attitude might make the child form a poor opinion about the other boy. While comparing the children, the parent is doing faulty upbringing of the good child.
5. The praises and commendations of the child must be within certain limits. Excess of these might make the child proud and conceited.

Imam 'Ali, The Commander of the Faithful, says:
"Lots of people develop conceit for the reason of praises heaped on them."[296]
"Don't exaggerate in praising others."[297]
One very good tool for effective upbringing and training is giving of rewards. Rewards are not a bad method of encouragement if they are spontaneous and not in fulllment of an earlier promise that if the child achieved a certain thing, he would be given a particular gift. If promises are made to the child beforehand, it might have negative impact on him. The child starts expecting a gift for every good thing

---

[296] Bihar al-anwar, v 72, p. 295

[297] Gharar al hukm, p. 209

he does. This will become a sort of gratication and the child would not strive to do better if these gifts stop forthcoming.

A person should have the habit of doing good deeds. He should do them to please Allah and serve mankind and not with an eye on the probable material rewards. If the child gets used to receiving gifts for every small reason, he might become narrow minded and selsh. He may not think it his duty to do anything for others, unless he gets something in return for his efforts.

He will try to escape from doing anything for others, as far as possible. This attitude is a very big fault in a person and the society. The rewards for any good work to the children, therefore, should be few and selective that receiving such gifts don't become a second nature for them.

When a child gets into the habit of doing tasks with his own initiative, reduce the frequency of gifts and rewards. Encourage him to do the work. Many parents give gifts to their children getting higher grades at their examinations. This way they encourage them to work harder at their studies. Perhaps this method is effective to some extent.

But there is a big defect in this. That it affects the child's sense of responsibility. The child works hard at his studies only because he wants to get the gift by obtaining higher grades. Otherwise, he would not bother to work hard. For everything he does, he expects a gift in reward for that.

One person writes:

"I was admitted to the fourth standard of a Religious School. I was very poor at the recitation of the Holy The Holy Qur'an. But my other class-mates were very good at their recitation. In the very rst class I attended, the teacher asked me kindly, "Can you recite the Holy The Holy Qur'an?" I replied nervously, "No, Sir. "He rejoined, "Don't worry, I shall give you the lessons. I know you can become one of the good students in the class.

Whatever doubts you may have, don't hesitate to ask me. These kind words of the teacher encouraged me and I started working with determination on my studies. By the end of the year I excelled at recitation of the The Holy Qur'an. I reached such a degree of prociency that in the absence of the teacher I was asked to conduct the class. I was also made responsible for reciting verses from the The Holy Qur'an at the morning assembly before commencement of the classes"

One girl writes in her memoirs:

"My father was a progressive person. One day, when my mother was away, he invited some of my teachers for the meal. He brought the ingredients for cooking and gave to me. I started to work in the kitchen with enthusiasm. In the noon Dad arrived with his friends. When I poured the victuals in the dishes, I noticed that they were not cooked properly.

The chicken was half done and the rice has become slushy with excessive water added while cooking it. All this was because, I had not properly learned the art of cooking. I was very worried. I was expecting a reprimand from my Dad at any moment. But contrary to all my expectations, Dad praised me in front of his friends. He said, "This food has been cooked by my darling daughter. It is so tasty!"

The guests too assented in agreement and praised me for my effort. Later on my Dad gave me a pat on my back. This word of encouragement enthused me to start earnestly at learning the culinary art. Today I am an expert at preparing lots of very good dishes."

www.ingramcontent.com/pod-product-compliance
Lightning Source LLC
LaVergne TN
LVHW091713070526
838199LV00050B/2385